The Progress of Revelation in the Old Testament

The Progress of Revelation in the Old Testament

Gerard Van Groningen

Resource *Publications*

An imprint of *Wipf and Stock Publishers*
199 West 8th Avenue • Eugene OR 97401

PROGRESS OF REVELATION IN THE OLD TESTAMENT

ISBN: 1-49824-844-6

Cataloging-in-Publication Data:

Groningen, Gerard van.

Progress of revelation in the Old Testament / Gerard Van Groningen.

viii + 76p.; 23 cm.

ISBN: 1-59752-629-0

1. Bible—Study and teaching. 2. Revelation—Biblical Teaching. I. Title.

BS591 G76 2006

Manufactured in the U.S.A

Contents

Preface

THIS COMPARATIVELY short book was written five decades after I began a serious study of the Scriptures, particularly of the Old Testament. When studying in seminary and graduate institutions I was introduced to the various higher critical schools of thought regarding the Scriptures. I began my in-depth study of these schools of thought that seemed to detract from the authenticity and reliability of the recorded Word of God. Two issues in particular engaged me. Did God, the sovereign covenant Lord, actually communicate with men in human language? And did this Lord actually enable men to infallibly record in writing what he had made known to them? These questions challenged me as a theological student. The result was that I increasingly realized that unless I had confidence that the Scriptures were authentic, authoritative, and wholly reliable I would not have the certainty and conviction needed for preaching and teaching truths that I and all other sinful persons required for the assurance of the forgiveness of sin, salvation and God-honoring service.

This book is, in a real sense, my answer to the questions I wrestled with initially. It is a testimony to the assurance and peace I had as I taught in Christian educational institutions.

My prayer is that readers will be blessed as I was.

G. Van Groningen
Autumn, 2004

I

Stating the Case

I. Introductory Comments

A. Agreement

There is general agreement among scholars and readers of the Old Testament that what is recorded in it can be referred to as revelation. Simply stated, people agree that the term revelation is the proper term when referring to the content of the Old Testament. Revelation occurred when there was a revealing of what was in the mind of our Triune God. To reveal is to uncover what is hidden. It is to open up the mind and heart by expressing what is in them. This content that is expressed is revelation when it is not known before the opening up or revealing activity took place. To sum up, one could say that revelation refers to that what is new or unknown. It had not been made known, nor apprehended nor considered before it was made known.

B. Disagreement

1. The Situation

There is much disagreement among scholars who have concentrated their study on the Old Testament, particularly on the subject of revelation. It must be emphasized that history and personalities involved in the historical process as such are not the basic reasons for disagreements. The disagreements are in the areas of how to consider the origin of the Old Testament and the interpretation of what the text presents.

There are basically three positions taken. They are not always clearly discerned because each position is not always clearly presented. When considering the message of the Old Testament, what should be considered as the initiating factor in the "revelation" recorded in the Old Testament? Is it God speaking the Word? Or is it God acting in time and space, the deed? Or is it the human awareness of and response to historical events.[1]

2. The Initiating Spoken Word

The position taken in this study is that the revelation presented in the Old Testament was initiated when God spoke. The spoken word introduced the divine deed. Human personalities responded to the spoken word and to the act.

The biblical testimony is that real communication came from God to man.[2] This came *ab extra*. In most instances it can be seen that the Holy Spirit was present and active in either the cosmos or in the hearts and minds of recipients who received divine knowledge.

The biblical text presents overwhelming evidence that revelation was initiated by God revealing himself personally, his intents and purposes. Creation was initiated by God speaking. Genesis one refers to God "said" no less than ten times. God also blessed, that is, he gave his benediction on what came forth after he had spoken. Indeed, God performed wonderful deeds in his creation work. The deed followed the spoken word. Adam and Eve responded to God's creating and forming words. When God had said it was not good for man to be alone (Gen 2:18) and Eve was given to him (2:22b), Adam responded "this is bone of my bone . . ." (2:23).

Redemption was begun when God interacted with Adam and Eve in the garden after they had sinned. God initiated the conversation when he called, "Where are you?" (3:9). After Adam responded God spoke to both Adam and Eve. He also spoke to Satan, pronouncing a curse on him (3:14-15). He pronounced a mitigated curse on Adam and Eve and carried out that curse on them and on the ground they were to rule over and cultivate.

A quick review of Scripture makes one realize how Yahweh God initiated conversation and action. God instructed Noah to build the ark (6:13-21), and told him to enter it (7:1). God told Noah, after he left the ark, to continue to obey the creation mandate (9:1-7). Yahweh said to Abram "Leave your country . . ." (12:4) and spoke to him again a number of times.

---

[1] In the ensuing discussion, the views of the many scholars who have written about these issues will not be considered. Rather, one individual who represents a specific position will be referred to briefly.

[2] Geerhardus Vos, *Biblical Theology* (Grand Rapids: Eerdmans, 1948) eleventh printing (1980) 12.

Yahweh called Moses from the burning bush (Exod 3:4). The Exodus and wilderness journey ensued. Yahweh God spoke to Joshua to succeed Moses (Josh 1:1-9). Samuel was called to serve as a prophet (1 Sam 3:4-14), and was commanded by God to anoint David (1 Sam 16:1). Yahweh God promised David an eternal house (2 Sam 7:11). Isaiah's prophecy records that "the Lord has spoken" (Isa 1:2). Jeremiah wrote that the word of Yahweh came to him, calling him to serve as a prophet (Jer 1:4, 11, 14). Ezekiel saw visions of God (Eze 1:1) and the Spirit said to him that he was to be sent to a rebellious people who were in captivity (Eze 2:28). Other prophets record that the "word of the Lord" came to them to serve (Hosea 1:1; Joel 1:1; Jonah 1:1; Micah 1:1; Zephaniah 1:1; Haggai 1:1; Zechariah 1:1). Amos (1:3) and Obadiah (1:1) record that Yahweh God gave them the message to prophesy. Nahum (1:1) and Habakkuk (1:1) received an oracle from Yahweh God.

The conclusion is very evident. Yahweh God initiated revelation by speaking to or giving his word to persons he had chosen to speak for him. They were to serve the people of the covenant. They were in need of instruction, guidance, and assurances. At this point it is necessary to refer to what was written before about the Holy Spirit initiating revelatory activity in the subjective aspect of people. Psalms and songs came from the hearts and mouths of people who were Spirit induced and led to do so.[3] God the Spirit thus gave revelatory messages through means of human abilities.

3. The Initiating Act

Are the activities that Yahweh God performed in history the initiating activities of biblical revelation? This question pertains particularly to Yahweh God's activities recorded in the Old Testament. In my early days of theological study, I first became aware that some Old Testament scholars were hesitant to consider Yahweh God's spoken word as the initiating factor in revelation as recorded in the Old Testament Scriptures. An Old Testament scholar had written a book entitled *The God Who Acts.*[4] He could be understood to say God's speaking was an act that biblical writers believed occurred. Wright, however, emphasized that objective historical facts should be considered as the source of revelation and theology.

Some points to be stressed are as follows. There should be no doubt that when God created the cosmos his speaking the creating word was and is an historical reality. It is factual, "God Spoke." This act of speaking was

---

[3] Ibid, 12.

[4] George Ernest Wright, *The God Who Acts*, (London: SCM, 1952).

the originating motivation of the act that followed. In various instances the act of speaking and the act of performing are so closely related that it is difficult to distinguish between them. God acted and performed as he spoke. He spoke and the action was originated.

The acts of Yahweh God are a tremendously valuable source for knowledge about God, his will, intentions, and abilities. Because this is reality, some schools of thought have expressed various views. One of these is the often referred to theme "Salvation History" or "Redemptive History.[5] There is also a tendency by many authors to consider the Old Testament Scriptures as basically a book of stories about events experienced by people. Indeed, it is important to know what happened but the truth to be emphasized is why what happened did happen? The answer must be: God had spoken and carried out his word by activities.

4. The Initiating Human Awareness and Response

There are various biblical scholars who insist that the message contained in the Old Testament was written as Scripture after human beings became aware of historical acts, deeds, or events.[6] Thus the Old Testament is strictly a human book written by keen observant men of historical activities past and contemporary. It should not be denied, or even ignored, that the Old Testament records human observations and responses to perceived historical events. But, to insist that men are to be regarded as the initiating agents of biblical revelation is to express opposition to what the Scriptures record. This opposition has its roots in philosophical and scientific presuppositions in which the divine dimensions of life, past and present, are considered irrelevant, if at all actual, influences.

In the study that follows it will be demonstrated that the Old Testament message was progressively revealed and recorded. God spoke, God acted accordingly, the human response to the acts of the words of God became the historical setting for further revelation.

---

[5] Brevard S. Childs indicates that he so understood Wright's position. Cf. *Biblical Theology of the Old and New Testaments* (Minneapolis: Fortress, 1992) 102.

[6] Gerhard von Rad in *Old Testament Theology*, translated by D.M.G. Stalker (London: Oliver & Boyd, 1962) is a basic representative of this position.

C. The Term Progress

1. The Term Explained

In the preceding paragraph the basic idea of how progress occurred is stated briefly. An illustration from nature may prove to be helpful. When one is in a fruit market and purchases fruit, e.g., a tomato or an apple, one acquires the end result of a process. The initial factor in the process was the seed. Without seed no plants appear. Rather, the seed planted in receptive soil, mulched, moist, and warm, sprouts and sends forth its plant. The seed produces a plant that in turn produces fruit, the actual tomato and apple and in the fruit is seed for subsequent planting. The spoken word is the initial seed, the seed develops and is active. It produces results that in turn produces the very same essential types of seed that was originally sown. There is no real progress; there is repetition. That is not the situation with the spoken word. The word produces growth and fruit which in turn provides the setting for new words, different words, that result in new activity and developed or new fruit.

When progress in revelation is observed then one sees and considers expanded or further revelation. One is not to think of the expanded and/or advanced revelation to be entirely new. In a sense nothing pertaining to the original was present. As will become evident in further study, there is advancement; there is development; there is growth; there is increasing richness as revelation continues from one stage to another or from one scene to another, or from one active situation to another.

2. The Progressive Phenomenon Demonstrated

In preceding studies this progressive revealing activity has been a major reality.[7] In these studies no specific and isolated study was made of the progressive dimension of revelation. Rather, Yahweh God was set forth as the sole source of revelation, providence, redemption and the application of these. In this brief study the emphasis will be particularly on revelation originating with Yahweh God and made known progressively from stage to stage, from, event to event, from recipient to recipient.

---

[7] Gerard Van Groningen, *Messianic Revelation in the Old Testament* (Grand Rapids: Baker, 1990; reprinted, Eugene, Ore.: Wipf & Stock, 1997). Reference henceforth to this study will be in *MROT* in the body of the manuscript. Three volumes with the title *From Creation to Consummation* (Sioux Center: Dordt, 1996–2004) will be referred to by *FCTC*, plus which volume and page(s).

II

Revelation in Creation

Moses, inspired by the Holy Spirit, recorded how and when God gave the initial revelation of himself in words and in the sovereign activities he performed (Genesis 1 and 2). The first two verses introduces these by recording that God began the entire process of revelation within the context of the cosmos that he had brought into existence. God's act of creating the formless, empty, dark, and deep watery mass-produced the setting in which the three-fold acts in the creation drama were performed. God spoke; God acted; God responded. Mankind had not yet been created; thus a human response was not possible.

I. Initiated by Divine Speech

The Psalmist, when praising Yahweh God, called for a joyful song to be sung to Yahweh. It was he who had spoken. By his word the heavens were made; also the starry hosts, the seas, the earth, the world and its people. All came to be and stood firm at Yahweh God's command (Psalm 33:1, 6-9). The Psalmist, understood to be David, repeated what Moses had written and reflected upon what he observed and experienced.[1]

A reading of Genesis one and two brings to mind the reality that Yahweh communicated his will, plan, purpose, and goal by speaking. The phrase "God said" is repeated ten (10) times in the two chapters (Gen 1:3, 6, 9, 11, 14, 20, 24, 26, 29; 2:18). God called, that is, named night, day, sky, land and seas (1:5, 8-9). He blessed, pronounced his good pleasure on the man and woman and the seventh (7) day (1:22; 28:2-3). Yahweh God also gave a verbal command regarding the tree of knowledge of good and evil (2:16-17).

If one takes the Scriptures seriously as Yahweh God's inspired revelation as authoritative and trustworthy, the inference is clear and posi-

[1] For a fuller discussion of Yahweh God's creation activities, cf. *FCTC,* 24–34.

tive. Yahweh God spoke, blessed, and commanded. So doing he brought the cosmos into existence *exnihilo* (from nothing). These divinely spoken words were the initiating means of Yahweh God's revelation. No one was there except the triune God. Only Yahweh God knew what was said and he had these initiating words revealed.

II. Progress in Revelation

The account of creation in Genesis one and two reveals two very important realities. First, it must be seen and accepted that Yahweh God's words were not mere verbal utterances. The divine words were spoken with ability and power. What God said became realities. As he spoke, he made, produced, separated, formed and made known the purposes and goals of what he spoke into existence.

Second, Yahweh revealed order as he progressed in his creating words and acts. For example, mankind, God's highest and most intricate created reality, was not spoken and brought into existence first. Rather, basic necessities for each created instance were produced first. Light and sky preceded seas and land. This set the context for the creating of all kinds of vegetation. These in turn required the light bearing celestial bodies—the sun and moon. These also regulated day and night. Then the context was ready for breathing and eating beings: animals for on the land and fish for in the waters. When the progress was completed; Yahweh God's image bearers, his vice-gerents, had the perfect environment in which to live and function obediently. Indeed, there had been progress in creation as progress in revelation had preceded each creation act. The final creation act was needed for mankind to perform his divinely given duties. The week was established—six days to work, one day to rest and worship.

III. God's Responses

Yahweh God had revealed by spoken words and the creative acts that followed each word that he was the Lord of the cosmos. And he did more. He revealed that he knew what had appeared, he evaluated all of it and concluded that all was good (Gen 1:10, 12, 18, 21, 25, 31). In reality he saw and declared that all that he had created, every aspect of the cosmos, including the man Adam and the woman Eve, was very good.

The term "good" must be properly understood. It means that whatever is referred to as good has met all requirements. There are (were) no defects or weaknesses. Every aspect—good—could fulfill the role that was intended for it by Yahweh God the creator. It meant that each aspect of the created cosmos had a purpose and a role in it. It meant that the cosmos, with all of its aspects, was a perfect, integrated unity.

Yahweh God's response to all that he had created was a revelation of himself as designer and maker. He revealed by word, deed, and response how his image-bearers were to function and respond to what they were to be, to do, and to contribute to the cosmos.

IV. Establishing the Covenantal Relationships

The term covenant does not appear in the first five chapters of Genesis. That must not be understood to mean that the idea of covenant was a later concept in the mind of God and in his revelation concerning his relationship with what he had created.[2]

The plain truth is that when God created the cosmos and his image-bearers, Adam and Eve, he established a relationship with them. Indeed, it was a relationship of creator and that created. It was a relationship of Lord and Master over the objects and subjects (people) he had placed as integral aspects of his universe. Yahweh God, however, did not withdraw as an aloof overlord. He maintained a living, loving relationship with all of his creation. The living, loving relationship was a bond that would not break or become ineffectual.

This covenantal bond is particularly revealed in the blessed reality that Yahweh God created man and woman in his image (Gen 1:27). Yahweh God made people to reflect him and to reveal him in finite ways. More, he made them and maintained a bond of love and life with them so that they could represent him in every sphere of life and cosmic aspects. Creating mankind in his image he made them royal. Men were made to be crown princes and women to be crown princesses and as such to rule over all other aspects of the created universe as vice-gerents. No absolute authority was given them but a divine bestowal of finite power and ability was given and revealed.

V. Instruction to Adam and Eve

Yahweh God instructed Adam and Eve in what he expected of them as vice-gerents. They were to represent him and exercise authority that he gave them. The text (Gen 1:28), informs us what Yahweh God did. He blessed them. He gave them his benediction. He gave them his commands which were in a real sense privileges and responsibilities. He revealed to them that

[2] Cf. my study of the covenant in *FCTC*, 24–25, 66; and *MROT*, 100–105. Cf. also references to M. Kline and W. Dumbrell, esp. in notes.

they were to increase; they were to have children. These were to increase also and thus fill the earth. They and their offspring were to subdue and rule over every aspect of the earth, sky and seas. This meant indeed that they had been given authority and responsibilities for their families, possessions and the environment in which they were to live, work and serve.

Yahweh God revealed to mankind that as they exercised authority and assumed their delegated responsibilities they were to consider the privileges given to them. They could consider all products, seed-bearing plants, to be their food. This meant they were expected to care for the plants and reap their seeds and fruit. Vegetation was provided as food for the animals.

Summing up, Yahweh God revealed that in the environment he had prepared, mankind was to have their home, perform their responsibilities and enjoy its privileges. Their greatest blessing was that they were made in God's image and were bonded to him in love for life. The images, i.e., the man and the woman, were also to reflect all the virtues that Yahweh God revealed concerning himself.

VI. Demonstrating Divine Virtues

The biblical text (Genesis 1–2) does not mention any specific virtue. Yahweh God did not out-rightly state that he had exercised any. He did however reveal some of these that are referred to in subsequent revelatory words and deeds. The Psalmist praises God for the wisdom he revealed in his creating work (Ps 104:24). In bonding himself as creator with his creation he demonstrated his love. In all of his creating activities he demonstrated his authority, power, ability and providential care. He revealed his glory and majesty (Ps 19:1; 81:9; 19; 89:5-8) and his uniqueness. God is incomparable (Isaiah 40:21-25).

Progress of Revelation in the Fall and Promise

Yahweh God's work of creation had been completed. Man and woman were created and placed in the heart of the created world, in the Garden of Eden. There the man and woman lived, fellowshipped with each other and with God. There they obediently served their creator and providential Lord. Revelation concerning all these events and conditions was completed. But although these were completed, further revelation concerning the created world with all of its inherent powers and possibilities was not only possible but to be expected. This was certainly true in regard to Adam and Eve. In fellowship with their creator and ever-providing God, they were in a position and condition to receive further revelation from their God in regard to their fellowship, service, goals and assurances of being well pleasing to God their loving Lord who had bonded himself to them in a lasting covenant relationship. Indeed, further revelation was given them regarding themselves and the cosmos in which they had been placed as vice-gerents.

I. The Edenic Context (Genesis 2–3)

A. God had Spoken

When Adam and Eve were placed in Eden and given their covenantal mandates, Yahweh God also gave them a prohibition. They were free to eat of every tree in the garden except one. To eat of this tree would bring tragic consequences. They would die (2:17). They would be removed from the scene of life with all of its attendant blessings. Mankind was given the glorious opportunity to be obedient and be submissive to their Lord. They had the potential for this as Yahweh God's image-bearers.

B. God Had Given a Helper

It has to be recognized that God's giving a suitable helper (Gen 2:20-22), was a great blessing for Adam. It was also a very important reality. Adam clarified his own relationship to this helper. In a real sense she was equal to him, bone of his bone, flesh of his flesh (2:23). She was made for him. Together they were image-bearers; together they had the honor of representing Yahweh God as the climax of Yahweh God's creating activity. They were both in the covenant bond with Yahweh God. They had been given a covenant bond between them, the marriage bond. This human marriage covenant was and is to be a reflection of the covenant between God and mankind.

In this edenic context, Yahweh God, having spoken, and having established a covenant bond between himself and mankind, further revelation was given. Previous revelation was not abrogated or to be ignored. Further revelation was given in the situation that developed.

II. Satan and the Antithesis[1]

Satan, the fallen archangel, entered the scene in paradise. He contradicted what Yahweh God had commanded regarding the eating of the tree in the middle of the garden (3:5). In disobedience to their covenant Lord, Adam and Eve ate of that tree. They immediately realized the consequences—nakedness and fear drove them into hiding. And when Yahweh God spoke to them, the marriage covenant came under tension and the covenant between Yahweh and mankind was broken but not irreparably.

A. Speech to Satan

Yahweh God spoke three times; first to Satan. He pronounced an absolute curse upon Satan. Yahweh God did more. He placed enmity between Satan and mankind, enmity that would never cease. Thus Yahweh God placed an absolute antithesis between Satan and mankind. Yahweh God continued his relationship as creator and provider of Adam and Eve and their posterity. Thus the good was maintained. Evil was pronounced as the diametric opposite. And the final crushing of Satan and evil was pronounced. Thus Yahweh God revealed that for all time the forces of good and evil would be in conflict.

---

[1] Cf. *FCTC*, Vol. 1, chap. 6, The Establishment of the Antithesis, 127–30.

B. Speech to Eve

Yahweh God addressed Eve. She had fallen first to Satan's snare. A mitigated curse was pronounced upon her. It was not a curse that would bring eternal separation from her creator Lord and her covenant bonded husband. The wonderful truth, in this sad context, was revealed. She would continue to be a seed-bearing woman. She would continue to have children but giving birth to them would cause increasing pain. And she, who had taken initiative wrongly (when she ate), was reminded that she had been given as a helper. She had failed in her God-given role by taking the initiative.

C. Speech to Adam

Yahweh God addressed Adam as the responsible person (3:17). He had listened to his wife and as the person who had been given responsibility to subdue and cultivate the earth, his task would be increased very much because the ground was cursed with a mitigated curse. It would continue to produce food. Adam would have to work hard and sweat to overcome the thorns and thistles that would grow. After a life of struggle and toil on the ground, he would be buried in it when he died. He could no longer expect to live continually in the garden of Eden (3:17-24).

Sin and the curse proved to be realities that would influence life on earth. Cain killed his brother Abel although he had been warned (4:6). The antithesis between good and evil came to a clear and powerful expression.

III. Yahweh God's Virtues Revealed

Yahweh God revealed additional virtues. He continued to have those he had revealed in his creating activity (Gen 2:4).

A. Omniscience

Omniscience was demonstrated Adam, trying to hide, did not affect God's ability to know what he had done. Yahweh God knew and he gave Adam the opportunity to confess his sin and guilt. Adam, however, did not confess but placed the blame on Eve. This was further evidence of sin and guilt.

B. Grace

Yahweh God revealed a deep and comprehensive love for his image-bearers. He did not punish Adam and Eve with immediate physical death and eternal condemnation. Divine love revealed and extended to guilty Adam and Eve was grace. This grace had not been revealed or demonstrated before. There had been no guilt. When Satan rebelled against God and was cast from God's presence, justice to its fullest extent had been revealed. Adam and Eve were likewise deserving of justice to its full extent. Justice, to an extent, was revealed when the earth was cursed and Eve's childbearing would be with pain. Grace, however, mitigated justice. God demonstrated his love for the guilty. He was gracious.

C. Mercy

Yahweh God's love for Adam and Eve was also demonstrated by his being merciful to them. When Adam and Eve realized that their God was coming they hid. They confessed that they were afraid (3:10). This fear made them miserable and uncomfortable.

Yahweh God revealed his love for them in their state of anxiety. He did not reveal his anger, much less his wrath against sin and the sinners. Rather, Yahweh God reached out to them in their wretched state of mind and heart. In a real sense he comforted them by not pronouncing wrath and immediate death. He acknowledged the sin and guilt of Adam and Eve by pronouncing the mitigated curse upon them. They would continue to live and be able to serve his purposes.

IV. Continuity of Life Was Assured

Yahweh God's love for his image-bearers and vice-gerents was revealed by means of an assurance that was eloquently expressed. He spoke to them regarding seed. They would not only be receiving grace and mercy, they would also be able to produce seed—progeny. Not only would they continue to live for a while, they would be bearers of continued life.

In this promise of life assured they were given the plan of the future. Satan and his followers would be crushed. Mankind's seed would be bruised – deeply hurt and suffer pain that could and would be endured. So, as mother Eve and her succeeding daughters would suffer pain in bringing forth seed, the seed would itself suffer pain. Yahweh God revealed another dimension of his covenant with mankind.

The covenant of redemption was instituted. Yahweh God, in love, grace, and mercy, added a dimension to his covenant of creation. Within this covenant of redemption, life would be continued within the all-inclusive covenant of creation.[2] Mankind would continue to be bonded to God as vice-gerents in creation and this bond was assured by means of the covenant of redemption. Redeemed mankind would continue as Yahweh God's

---

[2] Ibid, cf. 113, 133, 505.

image-bearers and as vice-gerents. And as revelation progressed, it would be clarified that this continuing of mankind's bond to Yahweh God by the covenant of redemption, within the broader dimension of the covenant of creation, would be assured by the crushing of the heel of the woman's seed.

V. Human Response

The response of Adam and Eve indicated they received Yahweh God's assurance of continued life. Adam and Eve had children. The antithesis, however, was a continuing reality. In the context of Adam and Eve's renewed obedience to Yahweh God Satanic influence and power was demonstrated by Cain's murder of his God worshiping brother Abel (4:2-12). The antithesis became more pronounced. Cain and his wife had a progeny. Adam and Eve had heirs via Seth. This human response in time became the setting for further progress of divine revelation.

IV

Progress of Revelation in the Time of Noah

I. Yahweh God Spoke

A. In Context of Violence

1. Wickedness Increased

The seed of Cain gained dominance in the then known world (Gen 4:17-24). There were also righteous men (4:24-25). They called on the name of Yahweh their Lord. The antithesis became more dominant and in time wickedness increased to such an extent that Yahweh said his Spirit would not strive or contend continuously (6:3). He said he would wipe mankind from the face of the earth. Animals and birds would be also. Mankind's sin brought death and ruin over that what he had to subdue and rule over (6:5, 11).

2. The Covenants Upheld

The broader covenant of creation included the redemptive covenant. Yahweh God did not forget nor forsake these covenants. He continued them with Noah, his wife, his sons, and their wives.[1] The bond of life and love established with creation and Adam and Eve was not broken. Note should be taken that not only Noah's family but also representatives of all living creatures were included (6:18-21). The text records that Noah was a righteous man. He obediently lived within the will of God. He lived a blameless life as he lived in communion (walked) with God.

---

[1] The NIV text does not have a correct translation of the Hebrew term that should be translated "I will cause to continue my covenant" (Gen 6:18).

A. Noah's God-given Mandate

1. Build

Yahweh God spoke to Noah. He gave him instruction on how to build an ark. It had to be of water resistant cypress wood. The capacity was to be such that Noah's family, their food, and representatives of all animals could be in it and food for them also. This Ark was to serve as the means of preservation and escape from the judgment Yahweh God was going to bring upon the earth. Noah was to become an agent of salvation and continued life for mankind and animals. He was to be a covenant agent representing his covenant Lord.

2. Response

Noah did everything just as God commanded him (7:1). Noah and his family entered the ark. Animals and birds did also. Note that this is stated emphatically (7:13-16). Noah's response to his Lord demonstrated his righteousness and his continued fellowship with his covenant Lord. And Noah's obedient response was the context for Yahweh God's revelation.

II. The Covenant Upheld

A. Death

Yahweh God had announced to Adam that death would be the result of sin. In Noah's time, in the midst of a world that had become very sinful, wicked, and guilty, death came to mankind and most of the earth. Indeed, Yahweh God upheld his redemptive covenant. There was a twofold outworking of the covenant. One was death. It was the irreparable break of the bond with God the Lord of life. It resulted in eternal separation from life on earth and especially from God. Both physical and spiritual separation from God the source of life and its blessings was the unavoidable result of sin.

B. Salvation

In the context of the curse being executed –the flood- Yahweh God demonstrated that his plan of salvation was upheld. In reality, the contrast is stark. In the context of judgment, covenant love, grace and mercy shone brightly. The ark was a means of salvation and preservation. Sin, wickedness, violence, and immorality had tragic influences. Yahweh God had his way of dealing with them. And doing that his salvation and preservation work demonstrated that Satan and his followers did not thwart him.

III. The Seed Indicated

A. Covenant Renewal

Yahweh God, when mandating the construction of the ark, assured Noah that his covenant with creation and the redemptive covenant were maintained (Gen 6:18). Yahweh God was faithful to his word. Noah had obeyed. The curse and grace, essential aspects of the redemptive covenant, had been revealed and demonstrated by Yahweh. Adam and his family had responded as required. These activities provided the context for Yahweh God to assure his covenant would continue to stand firm. He spoke to Noah and his sons saying "I now assure you that my covenant with creation and in that context of the redemptive covenant, will continue unshaken and steadfast" (9:9-13, 15-17).

Consider the assured promises Yahweh God made to Adam, his sons, and their progeny. They were to multiply, they would rule (fear of them), have food, protection from blood shed, no universal flood again, a rainbow to assure that the covenant was firmly established and this inclusive covenant would stand and hold forever throughout all generations (9:1-17).

B. Three Sons

Noah's three sons had been saved and preserved in the midst of the execution of the curse upon all creation and its inhabitants. These three sons became the progenitors of all families, tribes, races, and tongues (9:18-19). Then, in the context of the abuse of natural gifts (Noah's drunkenness), Noah prophesied concerning his sons Ham and Shem. The covenant curse was pronounced upon Canaan, Ham's son. Japheth was to be blessed with much territory.

C. Shem

Shem received a specific and particularly relevant prophetic blessing. This blessing must be understood, as assuring Noah, that through Shem Yahweh God's covenant would be perpetuated for all time. Thus Yahweh God revealed that Shem would continue the line of covenant fathers. Scripture reveals that this line begun with Adam was continued with Seth, Enosh,

Kenan, Mahalalel, Jared, Enoch, Methuselah, Lamech, Noah, and Shem (9:5).

IV. Human Population

A. Increased

Scripture records that under Yahweh God's providence the descendants of Japheth, Ham and Shem increased. Each group found their territory in which to live and increase their posterity. The inspired text records that the clans of Noah's sons developed nations and spread over all the earth (10:1-32).

B. Divided

Noah's descendants did not remain a unified people. Their increasing numbers were evidently a reason for separating. The inspired text, however, reveals that pride and ambition was motivating the people to become dominant in the earth and thus ruling over it, controlling it and all inhabitants (11:1-7).

V

Progress of Revelation in the Patriarchal Period

I. Introductory Comments

A. The Context

Following the story of the building of the tower of Babel and its aftermath, the biblical account singles out the genealogical ancestry of Shem. The purpose was to reveal Abraham's[1] ancestry and heritage. Efforts to determine the precise span of time from Shem's receiving the covenantal blessing until Yahweh God called Abraham is difficult to determine. It can be stated with a degree of certainty that Seth's progeny increased rapidly in number. Note that fathers had their first son when thirty (30) plus years old and continued to live four hundred (400) to two hundred (200) years. Thus when Abraham was called to leave his country and family, the community had become large. From this community Yahweh God elected Abraham to serve in a specific and special manner: to be the *covenant agent.*

B. Recipients of Revelation

During the patriarchal epoch Yahweh God spoke or had his word come to Abraham twenty-five (25) times. It is recorded that the angel of the Lord also communicated Yahweh's word to Hagar (Genesis 16:1-11), to Lot (19:1) and to Abraham (22:11, 15). Isaac did not receive direct revelation but his wife did concerning her unborn sons (25:23). Jacob received direct revelation (28:13-15; 31:3; 32:24-30; 35:1, 10-13; 46:2-4). Yahweh God spoke through Jacob when he blessed his twelve (12) sons (49:1-27). The inspired record of Jacob's son Joseph does not include a reference to Yahweh God speaking directly to Joseph. It does record that Yahweh was with Joseph

[1] The name Abraham will appear throughout this study.

and gave him success (39:1, 3). This lack of direct communication did not detract from Joseph becoming and serving as an important covenant agent. Joseph was not a physical ancestor of Jesus Christ (Judah was) but in his experiences and service he was an illustrious type of Christ.

C. The Organic Character Highlighted

The organic character of revelation shines through Yahweh God's words to and deeds for Abraham's forebears. It, however, is revealed in Yahweh God's interaction with the patriarchs reviewed in the preceding paragraph. At this point it is important to understand what is meant and referred to when calling attention to organic revelation. Consider what an eminent biblical theological author has written.

"The organic progress is from seed form to the attainment of full growth; yet we do not say that in the qualitative sense the seed is less perfect than the tree . . . in the seed-form the minimum of indispensable knowledge was already present."[2]

If one understands this organic character of revelation, one realizes that what was communicated to Abraham and expanded was not new—that is, the essential aspects were not new. What could be considered new revelation is what was added to, expanded and applied. Applying this to revelation in the Patriarchal epoch, one sees that the concepts of divine providence, of the covenant, of the seed of the covenant, the blessing and curse of the covenant, having been originally revealed, are given a fuller (not fullest) expression.

D. The Process

As the study of Genesis 12–20 proceeds the process becomes more and more apparent. Yahweh God's word is given. Often it is accompanied by a divine act. The spoken word is addressed to some person(s) and divine action follows to which there is a response. To be re-emphasized is that not the divine action (unless speaking is so considered) nor the human response initiates revelation or redeeming activities. There are scholars who have worked with the presupposition that the Scriptures are a record of human insights, perceptions, initiations and activities. The human aspect is considered to be the dominate factor. That is, that in the course of life, men observing what was happening conjectured that what they saw and experienced could have been influenced by powers beyond them. To make their conjectures plausible, men wrote that God saw, said, and did.

[2] Cf. Vos. *Biblical Theology*, 7.

II. Revelation to Abraham (Genesis 12:1—23:20; 25:1-16)

A. Yahweh God's Repeated Initiatives—The Spoken Word

Scripture records that there were various specific episodes relating Yahweh God's speaking to and interacting with Abraham.

1. Genesis 12:1-3

Yahweh God called Abraham and commanded him to leave his country, his people, and family. There were spoken reasons for his leaving. He was not immediately told where he had to go but he was promised blessings as his progeny became a great nation. He was promised fame and renown among his fellowmen. He was promised to be a source of blessing to all people. He was promised blessing if antithetical forces cursed him.

2. Genesis 15:1-19

Yahweh God assured Abraham of five great gifts. First, Abraham was assured that he would be protected, shielded, and rewarded in the midst of a developing hostile environment. Second, Yahweh promised seed in spite of Sarah's seeming infertility; his descendants would be numerous. Third, Yahweh God assured Abraham of a great spiritual benefaction: righteousness. Fourth, Yahweh God promised that Abraham would possess the land to which he had been led. Finally Yahweh God repeated his covenant bond with Abraham in a vision that included a dramatic scene and action.

3. Genesis 16:7-9

Yahweh God appeared as the Angel of the Lord to Hagar. She, pregnant with Abraham's son, was promised numerous seed.

4. Genesis 17:1-22

Yahweh God, in the context of having made a promise of much seed to Hagar, confirmed his covenant with Abraham. He did not make a new covenant. He added stipulations. Abraham was commanded to walk with God and lead a blameless life. He would be enabled to do so because he was assured that his covenant Lord was almighty. But Abraham was exhorted to keep and obey the covenant. And his seed—his progeny—were also to do so. Then Yahweh God gave further revelation. Abraham and all male seed were to be circumcised. This was to be a sign and seal of being bonded to Yahweh. For this bond to be truly real and ratified, blood had to be shed by the drawing of blood from the male's life initiating bodily organ.

In this context Abraham was reassured that Sarah his wife would bear a son with whom the covenant would be continued.

5. GENESIS 18:1, 13, 18-33

Yahweh God appeared to Abraham when three men also appeared. Abraham was again assured that Sarah, past the normal childbearing age, would have a son in spite of her disbelief. Yahweh also assured Abraham that in the midst of judgment upon wicked Sodom and Gomorrah, few though that the righteous might be, they would be spared.

6. GENESIS 20:3-7

Yahweh God revealed himself in a dream to king Abimelech to instruct him not to make Abraham's wife his concubine but to return her to Abraham. This must be considered Yahweh God's further revelation that Abraham and Sarah were to serve as covenant parents to the divinely promised seed.

7. GENESIS 22:1-18

Yahweh tested Abraham as a covenant agent. He was commanded to sacrifice his only son Isaac. When Abraham was about to plunge his knife into Isaac, Yahweh God prevented him. Abraham was assured that Yahweh God could and would supply a substitute: a ram was there. Abraham was again promised that his seed would be numerous, be blessed with cities and that all nations on earth would be blessed because Abraham obeyed.

B. Yahweh God's Actions Following His Spoken Word

The inspired text records that Yahweh God did as he spoke and promised. Abraham was led to Canaan. It is important to understand why. If Abraham had remained in Mesopotamia, in an area where the two great rivers, the Tigris and the Euphrates, watered the earth, causing prosperity to flourish; he would not be living in the area where he could be a source of blessing to all nations. He was living in the eastern part of the then known world. Yahweh God led him to where he would be in the midst of the entire then known world. Egypt, (Africa), was to the south and west; Asia Minor and Europe to the north and west, and Asian countries to the east. To reach

Europe or Asia, people from Egypt had to travel through Canaan and vice versus. The Mediterranean Sea was to the west by which far away countries could be reached by ship.

Yahweh God watched over Abraham. He revealed this by inflicting Pharoah and his household with a serious disease (12:17). Abraham received wealth, livestock, gold and silver (12:16; 13:1). Yahweh blessed Abraham when Melchizedek met him (14:18-20). He providentially removed Lot from Abraham's household and preserved him when Sodom and Gomorrah were destroyed.

Yahweh God confirmed and sealed his promises concerning covenant blessings. He was Abraham's shield (protector), and placed himself as surety for his future (great reward, 15:1). A great progeny would arise from a son (15:4). The covenant was symbolically sealed when Yahweh God, as a flaming torch, passed between sacrifices that Abraham had been instructed to provide (15:8-20).

In the episode that relates Abraham's interaction with Hagar, Yahweh God's word to her became a reality. Yahweh heard of Hagar's misery and assured her of a great future for her son to be named Ishmael, meaning God has heard you (16:11). Thus God honored Abraham by blessing his son to be born "illegitimately" to him by Hagar. Yahweh upheld his word to Abraham that he would be blessed with much seed (cf. also 17:19-20; 21:8-21).

Yahweh God's word brought judgment upon Sodom and Gomorrah. Yahweh God led Lot and his daughters to safety because he "was merciful" to them (19:15). His threatening word became a reality. As he had warned, Yahweh rained down burning sulfur, destroying the cities (19:24-26). Yahweh remembered his word too in answer to Abraham's pleading on behalf of Lot (18:16-33).

The grace of Yahweh God was revealed in the course of Abraham's interaction with Abimelech, king of Gerar. Abraham had not been truthful to the king concerning Sarah his wife. Abimelech had taken Sarah. The Lord warned the king concerning judgment to come (death) for taking Sarah. God prevented Sarah from being violated (20:6) and he had her returned to Abraham. In spite of Abraham's fear and hiding the truth concerning Sarah, Yahweh God's promises concerning land and blessings were repeated. He moved Abimlech to give Abraham freedom to live in the promised land and gave him additional wealth (20:14).

Yahweh God's revelation progressed when Isaac was born. He was gracious to Sarah "for he did what he had promised" concerning a son for Abraham and Sarah (21:1). According to Yahweh's assurance of seed to come via Sarah, Hagar and Ishmael were sent away because they were not part of the program concerning the promised seed. Yahweh did provide for him because he was Abraham's son (21:11-29).

In a very unusual manner Yahweh God tested Abraham by commanding him to offer Isaac as a sacrifice upon an altar. According to his word, Abraham needed not fear because God provided a ram as a substitute for Isaac.[3] In this account Yahweh God revealed his grace, mercy and providence in a spectacular manner (22:1-2, 11-18).

In summary of how revelation progressed in the time of Abraham, a number of factors stand out. The covenant, made known to Abraham's ancestry, was particularly and specifically confirmed with Abraham and his seed. Yahweh God 's dealings with Abraham and Sarah revealed his omnipotence and sovereignty. Nations were led and directed to be subservient to Abraham and that in turn gave Abraham the context to be a blessing to all nations. In spite of Abraham's weaknesses, he and his seed were graciously prepared to be Yahweh God's covenant agents in service to all nations.

The account of Yahweh God's spoken words to Abraham and how Yahweh's words issued into actions is not complete. The response of Abraham must be considered as integral to what Yahweh God said and did.

C. Abraham's Response

A consideration of the account of Yahweh God's revealing himself, his word, his plan, and his goal, to the extent that he did to Abraham and his fellowmen, must include a review of Abraham's responses.

Abraham acknowledged the sovereignty of God. He verbally expressed this when Yahweh God assured him he had no reason to fear and that there was a great future for him in regard to his seed and land (15:2, 8). Abraham confessed that he knew God had authority and power as sovereign over the universe and all that was in it.

Abraham believed. He had faith. This is stated eloquently in Genesis 15:6. In response to the promise of seed that would assuredly come, Abraham believed and was credited with righteousness. By faith Abraham was righteous (i.e., within the will of God). The book of Hebrews records that it was by faith that Abraham went and did as Yahweh God called and instructed him (11:8-17).

Abraham obeyed Yahweh God. The term obey does not appear often in the Scriptures. It does appear in important contexts. The Angel of the Lord, who was God, the second person, spoke as God to Abraham after

[3] Cf. my discussion of the ram, not Isaac, as a type of Christ, *MROT,* 144–45.

he had proceeded to prepare for the sacrifice of Isaac, said "because you have obeyed me" (22:15). Later when Yahweh God spoke to Isaac he again said "because Abraham obeyed me" (26:5).[4] The term obey, however, expressed how Abraham responded when called to leave his country (12:14). Abraham heeded Yahweh God's repeated promise concerning the land by taking possession of it (14:13-18).

Abraham, obeying his covenant Lord, also submitted to him. Obedience, characterized by submission, expressed trust and full reliance on his Lord. He knew and believed that "God could raise the dead" (Heb 11:19).

III. Revelation to Isaac

Isaac, the promised covenant son of Abraham and Sarah, had an important role in Yahweh God's plan for the continuance of his covenant with Abraham's seed. He had submitted to his father when he was told God would provide a sacrifice on Mt. Moriah (Gen 22:8-10). Isaac also submitted to his father by not taking a Canaanite woman as wife (24:3-4). He accepted Rebekah who was brought to him (24:22-26; 25:20). The account concerning Isaac concludes by referring to Isaac inheriting Abraham's wealth (25:4).

IV. Revelation to and through Jacob

Jacob, often referred to as the deceiver, became an agent in Yahweh God's plan for his people, the descendants of Abraham. From before the time of his actual birth, Sarah's twin sons struggled within her womb. Yahweh informed her that she would bear the progenitors of two nations. One was appointed to rule over the other (25:22-23). As Yahweh God had said, Jacob, born after Esau, became the dominant one. He was chosen to be the covenant seed bearer. As Abraham and Isaac had been elected (not Ishmael), so Jacob the younger one, inclined to deceiving others, was the one to whom Yahweh God continued to reveal his sovereign election and grace.

Yahweh God appeared to Jacob when he was fleeing from Esau. He received confirmation that the covenant promises given to his grandfather Abraham were for him (25:13-15). Jacob vowed that as these promises were realized he would give one tenth of his wealth to the Lord.

---

[4] The Hebrew text has the term *sama* that basically means to hear. If the verb is followed by the term *leqol*—to the voice, the thought expressed is obey.

Yahweh blessed Jacob with twelve sons and with wealth when in Laban's service. Yahweh wrestled with Jacob when he fled (32:22-31) but was assured that he had "overcome" in his struggle with God and man. Yahweh blessed him again (32:29). The covenant was again confirmed with Jacob when he had returned to the promised land (35:9).

Yahweh's grace was again manifested when he protected Joseph and led him to Pharoah's court. There Joseph proved to be the intercessor on behalf of his brothers. Joseph served as a type of Jesus Christ but it was Judah, the adulterer (Gen 38), who Yahweh God chose, as spoken prophetically by Jacob, was to be the ancestor of Jesus Christ, the true eventual covenant Lord and Redeemer (49:8-12).

V. Concluding Comment

The inspired text, Genesis 12–50, reveals that Yahweh God continued to reveal himself as the covenant Lord of his chosen agents, Abraham, Isaac, Jacob, Joseph and Judah. His covenant promises were upheld. He progressively revealed who would be his specific agent on behalf of all of Abraham's progeny. But specific blessings, through Abraham and his immediate descendants would be available to all the tribes, tongues, peoples and nations. Yahweh revealed progressively how the ones he chose were to be his servants on behalf of all peoples. Thus Yahweh God progressively revealed his sovereign plan for his chosen servant people and beyond them to all people.

VI

Progress of Revelation in the Mosaic Period I

I. Introductory Comments

A. The Biblical Account of the Mosaic Period

This is presented in four Penteteuch Books—Exodus, Leviticus, Numbers, and Deuteronomy. There is much material in these books that could be included in this study. Not all of this will be considered, rather the main elements that indicate progress in revelation will be.

B. The Word, Deed, Response Pattern

It must be stressed that in the accounts presented, the historic context included human responses that arose from people who had become slaves. The Israelite people had become numerous while in Egypt. Thus the stage was set for Yahweh God's spoken word and miraculous deeds. Then the human response came again. In most instances human responses to various divinely controlled situations set the context for Yahweh's spoken word and deed to which human responses followed.

C. The Covenant Upheld and Administered

References will be made to the Covenant. These reveal that the covenant made and confirmed from the time of creation and the revelation of redemption to Adam, and to Noah and the patriarchs was upheld and progressively administered. Judah's role was upheld. The covenant was administered providentially during Israel's time in Egypt and the wilderness. The progress of revelation, the subsequent divine activities and the human responses will be indicated in the study of four major themes in the four Penteteuchal books.

II. The Call of Moses, his Preparation and Task

Moses was chosen by Yahweh God to be Israel's leader. He was uniquely spared when other male babies were killed. He was prepared for his task in the home of his parents, in the palace of Egypt and in the wilderness to which he had fled after killing an Egyptian slave driver (Exodus 1–2). While serving as a shepherd he was called. God spoke to him from the burning bush. Moses was informed that the God of the patriarchs knew Israel's situation. The time had come for their deliverance. Moses was commanded to go to Egypt to bring the people out and to lead them to worship Yahweh God (3:1). God revealed himself as Yahweh when Moses hesitated (3:14). Signs of divine omniscience and omnipotence followed Yahweh's spoken command and promise to be with him.

Yahweh commanded Aaron to assist Moses (4:27). They gathered the elders of the enslaved people and Aaron served as spokesman to them but together they told Pharoah of their commission (6:28-30). When Pharoah refused, Yahweh God spoke to Moses saying that he remembered his covenant with the patriarchs and repeated his command to Moses to go to Pharoah in Egypt (6:1-12). Yahweh God's spoken words were followed by his miraculous actions: the ten plagues (7:1—11:9).

Moses and Aaron obeyed. They confronted Pharoah who remained hardened under Yahweh God's hand. But Yahweh God sovereignly overruled. He spoke again, commanding Moses and Aaron to institute the Passover (12:1ff.). While the people responded Yahweh God slew all the first-born of Egypt.[1] This divine deed drew a response from Pharoah "Go, worship" (12:31).

Yahweh God's spoken words, his ensuing deeds and the human response are graphically presented in the account of Moses carrying out his task. The first-born were consecrated (13:1-16); the people were led to and through the parted Red Sea and the pursuing Egyptians were destroyed. The redeemed people responded in song led by Moses and his sister Miriam (15:1-21). Moses' task became awesome when water and food were needed. Yahweh God spoke and provided both (16:1—17: 7). He gave victory over the Amalekites under Moses and Joshua's leadership and wise counsel to Moses on how to administer leadership through Jethro (18:1-27).

In summary it should be clearly stated that there was considerable progress in Yahweh God's revelation during the initial time of the Mosaic period. Yahweh God's covenant was confirmed with an enslaved people.

[1] Yahweh God's carrying out his word, slaying the first-born, was done as the people responded celebrating the Lord's Passover. Note Exod 12:12 "On the same night I will pass through Egypt and strike down every first-born . . . ."

His sovereign authority and power were revealed over the greatest nation on earth at that time. Israel became a redeemed people. They were instructed on how to commemorate divine deliverance (the Passover). They were symbolically baptized as a people when led through the parted Red Sea. They were miraculously provided water, food, and victory in the desert. Yahweh God did indeed reveal tremendous progress in keeping his covenant with his chosen people.

III. The Theocracy: Exodus 19:1-25[2]

A. Yahweh Spoke

Yahweh God had revealed his faithfulness, authority, power and gracious providence. Israel, as a people, had been delivered from Egypt, marched through the Red Sea and led through the desert to Mt. Sinai. More revelation awaited the covenant people there. It was defining revelation.

Yahweh God, in words to Moses, referred to his purpose of redeeming the people and as a mother eagle carrying her young, had brought them to himself. Yahweh God thus established an intimate relationship with Israel. He went on to remind Moses that he was the sovereign Lord over the entire world. Israel had been chosen as a precious possession. Israel was to be a kingdom; they were to be a priestly nation among all nations. They were to be a holy people.

B. Yahweh Acted

Yahweh God thus confirmed his covenant with Abraham's seed. And in this confirmation he made it known that he was the Sovereign Lord who demanded obedience and full submission in keeping all the requirements of the covenant. They were to be consecrated to him. They were to approach him only when the trumpet sounded. Yahweh God also revealed his power over the natural world with a display of lightening, thunder, a thick cloud of smoke, and a trumpet blast. This revelation of the awesome character of Yahweh God was concluded by God speaking directly to the people. The biblical text also records that Yahweh God descended to the top of the mountain and called Moses to join him. Aaron also had to come up—but none of the people.

In chapter nineteen (19), one finds the inspired record of Yahweh God confirming his covenant with his people with words. Yahweh God

[2] Consult *FCTC*, Vol. I, 323–53, for an in-depth study of Yahweh God and Israel at Mt. Sinai and 358–395 for Yahweh God and Israel in the desert after Mt. Sinai.

carried out his word by deed. He established Israel as a kingdom over which he reigned in a unique and direct manner. He also established offices in the kingdom. Aaron was appointed as priest to represent all priests and all the people (19:24); a perpetual priesthood was later established (Lev 8). Moses was made his spokesman, a prophet (cf. Deut 18:14-20) and served in an administrative role. In reality, Yahweh was the king of Israel; Moses was his vice-gerent. This vice-gerent office remained until kings Saul and David were anointed

C. The People Responded

The response of the people should be noted. They received consecration (Exod 19:14); they washed their clothes. They trembled (19:16) and were led to meet God (19:17). The stage was set for Yahweh God to speak more. Moses and Aaron responded by initiating and carrying out their prescribed duties.

IV. The Commandments

The commandments Yahweh God gave from Mt. Sinai served as the basis for all further commandments, directives, and instructions for holy consecrated living under Yahweh's reign over the theocratic kingdom

A. The Decalogue

The ten (10) commandments covered three covenantal mandates.[3] The first four give instruction concerning mankind's relationship to God and worship. Commandments five through seven give instruction concerning the relationship of people with others. And commandments eight through ten give instruction concerning people's relationship with creation and culture. These three covenantal instructions are developed in varying degrees of detail (19:22—24:18). These instructions were not set out in a strict organizational manner.

B. The God-Man Relationship

Yahweh God called for offerings to be used to build a place, the tabernacle, for people to meet God (25:1-8; 26:1-37). He also called for the Ark (25:10-22), the table (25:23-30), the lamp-stand (25:31-40), the oil for it (27:20-21); and the altar of burnt offerings (27:1-19).

3 Ibid. Cf. the three covenantal mandates, 338–41.

Instructions regarding the priests were included (28:1—29:46). Specific instruction regarding the Sabbath was added (31:12-18), as were the Lord's instructions regarding anointing, oil (30:22-33) and the altar of incense that had to be made (30:7-10, 14-16).

The God-Man relationship was put to a serious test while Moses was on the mountain receiving instructions regarding matters of worship (32:1—34:9). The purpose of worship was to have the people express and rejoice in the worthiness of Yahweh God, to exalt him, to praise him and to develop the covenantal bond of love and life between their Lord and themselves. But the people demonstrated their immaturity and fickleness when Moses was not with them. They broke the covenant bond by erecting and worshiping a golden calf. Yahweh spoke threatening words. Moses prayed for forgiveness and reconciliation. The people expressed sorrow by stripping of their ornaments. Yahweh God forgave the people because Moses interceded. He then revealed his glory to Moses who made new tablets of stone that he presented to Yahweh God who renewed the covenant when he revealed himself as Yahweh the Lord, compassionate, gracious, slow to anger, abounding in love and faithfulness, maintaining love to thousands, forgiving wickedness, rebellion and sin. He will punish the guilty and their posterity (34:6-14) and he will remain a jealous God demanding obedience (34:11).

Once the relationship was restored, the covenant mandates were repeated and explicated (Exod 35:1—Num 10:10). Regulations concerning the Sabbath (35:1-3) were repeated and explicated numerous times. Instructions concerning the tabernacle and its "furniture": the ark, table, lampstand, altars, basin, and the courtyard were given (35:4—38:31); orders were given concerning the priests' clothing and paraphernalia (39:1-31).

The materials that were needed had been supplied when Yahweh God had made the Egyptians favorably disposed toward the people when they were asked to give silver and gold (Exod 11:2-3). The leaders in Israel had responded so that Moses was able to complete the tabernacle (Exod 40:31). Yahweh demonstrated his approval by having the cloud of glory cover the tabernacle.

The God-Man relationship was to be exercised by the sacrifices people were to bring (Lev 1:1—7:38). The priesthood was ordained (8:1-35). When the priests began their ministry in response to Yahweh's word and provisions, divine glory appeared to all the people when Aaron blessed them and they worshiped Yahweh (9:22-24). Not all went well, however, two of Aaron's priestly sons did not show themselves holy and died before the Lord (10:1—19).

C. The Man to Man and the Man to Culture Relationship

As aspects of life in Israel unfolded while at Mt. Sinai, further revelation was given concerning human inter-relationships and human interaction with cultural aspects. These two were often intertwined. Blood was forbidden to be used as food or offered to idols. Sexual purity was to be maintained. Instructions concerning daily life in the camp and eventually in the land were added. Rules for punishment were outlined, as were further duties of the priests, especially concerning sacrifices and the feasts. Disobedience resulted in death when a blasphemer was stoned (24:10-23; 26:14-39). Rewards for obedience to the three covenantal mandates were announced (26:1-13). Finally, Yahweh God demanded that vows of dedication be strictly carried out – regarding persons, animals, and possessions (27:1-29).

V. Final Activities at Sinai

Yahweh God spoke repeatedly to Moses and also to Aaron. Yahweh commanded Moses to take a census of the whole Israelite community and gave instructions on how to proceed (Num 1:1-4). It is recorded that Moses did so (1:19). Yahweh also gave instructions concerning the arrangement of the tribal camps and the people did everything Yahweh commanded (2:1-34). Yahweh gave instruction concerning the different groups in the tribes (4:1-40). He thus revealed he insisted on distinctions, order, and tasks.

Further instructions were given concerning purity in the camp and other social issues (5:1—6:21). Religious regulations and duties were prescribed (7:1—9:14). Two other specific matters are recorded. The Cloud over the Tabernacle was to serve as a traveling guide (9:15-23). Also, two silver trumpets had to be available for signaling assemblies and for gathering to celebrate feasts (10:1-10).

VI. Concluding Comment

The biblical record as presented in Exodus 1:1 through Numbers 10:10 concentrates on what Yahweh God revealed by his words. He revealed himself and his purposes for his chosen covenant people.

It must also be emphasized that Yahweh God acted after he had spoken. He did in accordance with his verbal revelation. The people responded as they heard and saw what Yahweh God did. Revelation progressed!

VII

Progress of Revelation in the Mosaic Period II

I. Revelation During the Journey in the Desert[1]

A. During the Initial Stage of the March

The cloud, signifying Yahweh's presence, lifted from above the tabernacle. The people had been organized for the journey according to Yahweh's instruction. Moses' request for Hobab to lead was not in order. He did submit to Yahweh God's leading (Num 10:35-36). Further revelation was given to Moses, Aaron and the twelve tribes as they traveled.

The complaint of the people due to hardship was the context for a demonstration of anger by Yahweh. Fires burned among them. Manna was continually provided (Exod 16:4, 31; Num 11:4), and as before meat (quail) was also given (Exod 16:13; Num 11:31). Moses was given aid in administration when Yahweh commanded him to select seventy men from among the elders in Israel who were divinely endowed by Yahweh with the Spirit who enabled them to prophesy for one time (Num 11:24-25). Joshua, who had served as an aide (Exod 17:9-14; 33:11), continued as such (Num 11:28-30). When Miriam and Aaron, desiring more authority among the people, sought to minimize the role of Moses because of his "foreign" wife, Yahweh formally established the office of prophet (Num 12:1-8) and it was re-confirmed later (Deut 18:15-22). Thus the three offices were functioning. Moses served as uncrowned ruler/king; Aaron was the priest and Moses also served as prophet.

Israel, as a nation, was to inherit the land promised to Abraham (Gen 12:1-3; 17:8). Yahweh instructed Moses to send men to explore the land

[1] There is disagreement among scholars who have prepared maps in which the precise way Israel followed on their journey through the desert. This possible uncertainty regarding the exact route does not affect what was revealed during the march to the Plains of Moab.

"I am giving to the Israelites" (Num 13:1-2). Ten men reported that the promised land was too fortified for Israel. Two believed that Yahweh would give victory. The people, however, rebelled and Yahweh threatened to "strike them with a plague" (14:12). Moses interceded and pled the covenant of grace (14:17-19). The rebelling people were punished; they, except Joshua and Caleb, would not enter the land.

B. During the Second Stage of the March

Although Israel was not to inherit the land for almost forty (40) years, Yahweh God assured them of eventual entrance into the land giving them instructions regarding offerings when in the land (Num 15:4-31). While in the desert, Sabbath laws had to be obeyed. Yahweh commanded that a Sabbath breaker be put to death (15:32-36). The people were commanded to prepare tassels which were to remind them of Yahweh's demand for obedience (15:37-40). In this context Israel was reminded by God that "I am the Lord your God who brought you out of Egypt to be your God . . ." (15:41).

The sincerity of the command to be obedient to Yahweh and to his representative, Moses, was demonstrated when Korah, Dathan, and Abiram challenged Moses' leadership (16:1-50). Yahweh destroyed the rebels and the men who were disobediently offering incense. In that context Yahweh God covered the Tent and revealed his glory. Aaron made atonement for the people who objected to the killing of the rebels. Aaron was confirmed in his role as priest when Yahweh commanded Moses to instruct the people that Aaron was to be honored. To substantiate this confirmation Aaron's rod produced almonds (17:1-12). This episode was followed by Yahweh instructing in further detail what the duties of the priests and levites were (18:1—19:22). Ceremonial cleansing was emphasized.[2]

Yahweh demanded obedience to his commands and ordinances. Moses was also to demonstrate this obedience. He failed to honor Yahweh when he spoke as if he was to supply water, he and Aaron were denied entrance into the promised land (20:1-13). Moses disrobed Aaron on Mount Hor and after Aaron's death his son Eleazar was inducted as a priest to succeed his father (20:22-28). Two more episodes were recorded in which Yahweh's revelation gave guidance; the destruction of Arad and the erection of a bronze snake for people to look to for healing (21:1-9).

In conclusion to the review of Yahweh God's continued revelation to his people in the desert it should be noted that the entire body of revelation was not given as a whole in one context. Yahweh revealed himself,

[2] An added duty of the priest was to offer a red heifer for cleansing (Num 19:1-20).

his purposes and who his agents were to be. As Israel, the people lived, marched, camped, and reacted to their desert environment and circumstances, Yahweh God continued to reveal himself as their covenant Lord who was to be obeyed and trusted in all circumstances. These provided contexts for further revelation. Yahweh God demonstrated throughout the entire desert experience that he was with his people, he knew their needs and met these. Thus his revelation progressed.

C. During the Third and Final Stage of the March

As in previous passages considered, so also in the passage under consideration in this section, these are repeated references to Yahweh God verbalizing his will to Moses and the people.[3]

Four episodes in which Yahweh communicated verbally are recorded. 1) Moses was commanded to gather the people so they could drink at the well, Beer (Num 21:16), and assured Israel that Og, king of Bashan would be defeated (21:24). 2) When Israel arrived on the plains of Moab, across the river from Jericho, Yahweh opposed Balak's attempt to curse Israel. He spoke, warning Balaam not to do as Balak requested (22:9, 12, 20). The Angel of the Lord, the pre-incarnate Lord, also confronted Balaam. A divine message was given to Balaam as to what he should repeat to Balak (23:16). It is also recorded that the Spirit spoke through Balaam (Num 24:2).[4] 3) Yahweh commanded that a census of the whole community of Israel be taken after a plague struck Israel for being seduced by Moab. Other instances of Yahweh speaking are as follows: regarding the inheritance of land for each tribe; Joshua to succeed Moses (27:12-25); offerings as prescribed before were to be properly carried out; vows were to be kept. (30:1-16); vengeance on the Midianites was to be executed; and instruction was given concerning spoils (31:1-54). 4) Detailed instructions were given concerning land for two and a half tribes on the east of the Jordan (32:1-42) and for Israel, when having crossed the Jordan into their promised inheritance.

In conclusion to this review of what Yahweh God revealed when Israel entered the eastern part of the promised land, it must be repeated that he was sovereignly in charge. He revealed his justice and faithfulness to his chosen people. They were never left to wonder or be perplexed about what

---

[3] It is difficult for some commentators to accept the written Word of God that repeatedly informs the reader that God communicated in words to his people. In the section now to be considered, the phrases "the Lord said" and "the Lord spoke" occur no less than twenty (20) times.

[4] For my detailed study of the Balaam/Balak encounter see *MROT*, "The Balaam Prophecies," 239–45. Cf. also *FCTC*, Vol. I, 401–6.

was to happen to them or what they were to do as step by step they entered the land and began to receive their portion of the promised inheritance.

II. Revelation Given on the Plains of Moab

A. The Role of Moses

Moses performed his duties as spokesman, leader and administrator in Egypt, the wilderness and during Israel's entrance into the land east of the Jordan River. It was on the plains of Moab that his role as prophet came to its fullest expression. The final words concerning Moses' role is recorded in the Book of Deuteronomy (Deut 34). Moses was unlike any other prophet. He knew Yahweh face to face who did miraculous signs and wonders with great power. Moses had his failings (3:23-27), and was not permitted to lead the people across the Jordan River nor permitted to cross himself although he saw the promised land from Mount Nebo. He did, however, speak Yahweh's will to the people immediately before they were to cross the Jordan River.

Moses served in an important role in presenting the unity of Scripture. His words as recorded in Deuteronomy form a uniting and integrating bond between the first four books of the Old Testament and what follows from Joshua onwards. He reviewed what Israel experienced once they had heard the ten commandments and the application of them during the wilderness journey. Speaking as a prophet, he also gave further revelation concerning Yahweh's will for Israel once they entered the land and settled in it.

B. Additional Aspects

Moses re-emphasized various commands and laws that Israel had received. After reviewing what Yahweh God had done for them he stressed the absolute necessity of obedience (Deut 4:1-40). The people were to remember what Yahweh had said to them and what he had done for them and these truths were to be taught to their children (4:9-10).[5]

It should be noted that it is not recorded very often in Deuteronomy that Yahweh God spoke to Moses, Aaron or the people. Moses repeated much that Yahweh had spoken and revealed in previous contexts. A new historical experience awaited the people. They were to cross the river and take possession of the entire land promised to Abraham.

---

[5] Later Moses urged the people to impress God's will upon the hearts of the children (Deut 6:7-9)

A select number of realities previously known were repeated with additional explanation. The ten commandments were repeated. These served as a substantial part of the covenant Yahweh God had made with Israel (5:2, 6-21). He reminded the people they had heard their Lord God and had seen his glory and majesty (5:24). The people's life-long response was to love Yahweh God with all their heart, soul and mind (6:4). Yahweh their God demanded that they demonstrate their love by obeying and serving him (6:10-25). That meant also that the nations presently occupying the land had to be driven out. No interaction with them would be permitted (17:1-26). Moses emphasized what Yahweh God asked of them " . . . to fear him, to walk in all his ways, to love and serve with all their heart and soul, and to observe the Lord's commands and decrees (10:12—11:30). This was to be to their good (10:13).

Israel was instructed regarding how they were to worship once in the land and to sacrifice (12:1—13:18), and to celebrate feasts (16:1-17). Social relationships were addressed (15:1-18; 16:18-20; 17:8-13) instructions concerning kings, priests and Levites were clarified (17:14—18:8), and regarding prophets to be raised up (18:14-22). Instruction from Yahweh also concerned Law Courts (17:8-13), cities of refuge (19:1-21), warfare (20:1-20), intermarriage (21:10-14) and other social matters (21:15—25:19), curses and blessings were pronounced (27:15—28:68). Covenant keeping was re-emphasized (29:1—30:20).

The Book of Deuteronomy concludes by referring to Joshua being appointed successor to Moses and Moses writing the law as presented verbally and giving the written law to be placed in the Ark of the Covenant (31:9-13). It is then recorded that Yahweh God spoke to Moses concerning his death (31:4-23), after which he wrote the Song of Moses (31:30—32:43). Yahweh also spoke to Joshua saying he had to be strong and courageous, that he would lead the people into the promised land. These words were concluded with the covenant promise, "I myself will be with you." (31:23-24). Then Yahweh God told Moses to go up to Mount Nebo to die (32:48). Moses, before going to Mount Nebo, blessed Israel (33:1-29). Moses was given a view of the promised land (34:1-4). Moses died; no person knew where he was buried (if indeed he was, cf. Matt 17:3).

Concluding comments: the Book of Deuteronomy reveals that Yahweh God had graciously and providentially fulfilled his promises to Abraham that his descendants would be brought to the promised land. Moses had his role. Joshua was introduced to succeed him. Yahweh God kept his covenant and the people had every reason to do so also.

VIII

Progress of Revelation during the Period from Joshua to David

After Moses died Joshua became Israel's leader and administrator. He inherited a full and rich store of revelation Yahweh God had graciously and wonderfully provided. Israel knew the promises, commandments, and directives on how to live in the land that they received as a gift from Yahweh. They had the abiding assurance that Yahweh God would be their God. He would be with them. He would care for them. His love would never be withdrawn from them.

I. Revelation in the Time of Joshua

The Book of Joshua begins with the statement that after the death of Moses "Yahweh God *said* to Joshua" (Josh 1:1). He repeated the promises concerning the land and that he would be with Joshua as he had been with Moses. Joshua was commanded to be strong, courageous, and to keep the Book of the Law before him for meditation and guidance (1:2-9).

Joshua took charge and as he did Yahweh God proceeded to encourage him by saying to him that he, Yahweh, would begin to exalt Joshua before the people to assure them that he was indeed Yahweh's appointed successor to Moses (3:7-8). When plans were made to cross the Jordan River Yahweh God spoke again instructing him to appoint twelve tribal representatives who were to take up stones from the middle of the Jordan (where the priests with the ark stood) to serve as a memorial for later generations (4:1-13). When Israel crossed the Jordan River safely Yahweh did as he had said, "he exalted Joshua in the sight of Israel who then revered him all the days of his life (4:14). At Yahweh's command Joshua commanded the priests to come up out of the river (4:15-17). It is striking that Joshua gave all honor to Yahweh God who had dried up the Jordan as he had the Red Sea for Moses (4:20-24).

A truth to emphasize: Joshua demonstrated that he was truly a type of Jesus Christ who, in a greater and deeper sense, would bring his people safely from this life to their eternal abode.

Yahweh God spoke to Joshua concerning the Israelites' need to carry out the sacrament of circumcision (prelude to New Testament baptism) and to celebrate the Passover. Note that when Israel was to be led from Egypt they celebrated the Passover. Once led into the promised land they did so again. And through Joshua the people were assured that their past (Egypt) was rolled away. With the celebration of the Passover, they were introduced to the food in the promised land. Manna, desert food, was not to be eaten anymore (5:1-12).

Another important revelation was given to Joshua. The greater Joshua, whom he typified, challenged him to be the humble representative of his triune Lord (5:13-15). He responded and under Yahweh God's command and leadership Jericho was captured (6:1-27). Thieves were exposed, Israel captured the strong cities and enemy armies (7:1—8:29). Yahweh led Joshua (cf. 8:18) and he kept and renewed the covenant as Moses had passed on Yahweh's revelation concerning this (8:30-35).

As the revelation of Yahweh God progressed, Joshua performed his duty as servant of Yahweh God leading the covenant people. Yahweh encouraged Joshua "not to be afraid" (10:7), because no enemy would succeed in opposing the people, Joshua or Yahweh God (10:9—13:7). The conquered land was divided; each tribe received an inheritance (14:8—19:51). To be noted: Yahweh God's promises concerning an inheritance for Caleb (14:6-15) and Joshua (19:49-51) were honored.

Yahweh God made provision for justice in the newly acquired land by instructing Joshua that "cities of refuge" had to be designated (20:1-9). Levites, in specific service to Yahweh, were given cities (21:21-45). When Joshua made his farewell speech he reviewed what Yahweh God had said and done. He challenged them to be faithful to their covenant Lord. They vowed they would (24:16-24). The covenant was renewed (24:25-27). Until after Joshua's death, and of the elders who served with him, the people were faithful to their sovereign covenant Lord.

Yahweh God's revelation by word to Abraham and through Moses and Joshua progressively given was progressively realized. When Joshua died and Yahweh's word concerning the past, present and future was spoken, Israel was a people richly blessed. They had every opportunity to develop into a national kingdom that could be a blessing for every tribe, people and nation on earth. Yahweh God's revelation given progressively throughout preceding generations had been realized in miraculous deeds performed by Yahweh, his appointed representatives and the leaders of the covenant people. The people themselves had been led to follow and serve—and they did in spite of some who rebelled and were removed from the community (cf. for example, Achan 7:1-26, and the Gibeonites 9:1-20).

II. Revelation in the Time of the Judges

Israel required leadership when they as a developing nation settled in the land. The twelve tribes, each in their allotted territories, had to be united. Yahweh commanded that Judah was to be a leader (Judg 1–2). Recall what Jacob had said of him in all cases (Gen 49:8-12).[1] Judah was successful; Yahweh God was with the men of Judah (Judg 1:19). The setting for years of trouble was developed when most of the tribes did not remove all inhabitants from the areas given them (1:22-36). The Angel of Yahweh, the pre-incarnate Christ, rebuked them. They were informed that difficult times were before them (2:1-5).

The people of Israel were afflicted and persecuted repeatedly. Judges, who became deliverers, were raised up (2:6—21:25). During this long period in Israel's history there was no defined progress in revelation. What Yahweh God did reveal was that he was fully aware of Israel's disobedience and rejection of his word. Various nations were led to dominate over Israel. Yahweh God intervened directly in a number of occasions. Gideon received advice (7:1-7), as did Jephthah (10:10-14; 11:29), Manoah and Samson (13:1—16:31).

The account related in the Book of Ruth gives additional information concerning life during the period of the Judges. There is no further verbal revelation. Israel had divine revelation given to them before. But Yahweh God, not recorded as having spoken, revealed how he directed the life of a man from Judah and his descendants (Ruth 1:1-2). The ultimate purpose was to continue the genealogical line from Judah to David (4:18-22).

III. Revelation Regarding Samuel

A. Introductory Comments

Samuel stood in the context of a major transition in the life of the nation of Israel.[2] He was a central agent in the transition of the period of the Judges to that of the kingdom. The kingdom reality to come had been revealed by

[1] The text records that Joseph did also. It is interesting to note that descendants of these two sons became rulers in Israel, and Christ came from one, Judah.

[2] Cf. *FCTC*, Vol. I, 475–79. "The Role of Samuel the Prophet."

Moses (Deut 17:14-20). While serving as the last Judge, Samuel anointed the first king. Judges would continue to function in a judicial capacity, not in an administrative or political position.

A second major transition occurred in the time of Samuel. Yahweh God had promised Moses that the office of prophet would become a functioning reality (Deut 13:12-22). He would put words in the mouth of prophets.[3] Samuel was the first to function in this official prophetic office. Progressive revelation would continue often in conjunction with the fulfillment of what had been revealed before. Thus there was a definite continuity in Yahweh God's word to his people.

B. Samuel's Role

Samuel was a child conceived with prayer and was dedicated to minister in the tent of Yahweh. The priest's sons were wicked and judgment was pronounced on Eli's family. It was Samuel's first message from Yahweh God. As Samuel ministered the worship and service in Yahweh God's place of "residence –the Ark" was cleansed and sanctified (1 Sam 3:1-7). Yahweh God's help in helping Israel was memorialized by the setting of the stone "Ebenezar" (7:2-17).

Yahweh God spoke to Samuel saying he should "give them a king" (8:22). Samuel anointed Saul saying that Yahweh had anointed him as leader over his inheritance (10:1, 21). Saul was confirmed as king by the people under the leadership of Samuel (11:14-15). But Samuel had to inform Saul that he was rejected by "Yahweh his God" for his disobedience (13:1-4; 15:1-35). A concluding statement records that Yahweh God was grieved that he had made Saul king.

Yahweh's care over Israel and concern for his covenant people was progressively revealed when Yahweh God spoke to Samuel when he mourned for Saul. He was sent to Jesse of Bethlehem to anoint one of his sons (6:2). He was instructed to approach Jesse and his sons with a sacrifice and not to consider outward personal appearances. Yahweh said he judged the heart. When the sons of Jesse appeared before Samuel, Yahweh commanded Samuel to anoint David (16:12). David was led to serve Saul for some years and thus gained experience in political and military affairs.

The last appearance of Samuel was in the cave of the witch of Endor. When he was called up to speak to Saul he informed Saul that he would die on the battlefield fighting the Philistines (28:16-19).

---

[3] Yahweh God had also revealed that false prophets would presume to speak in his name (Deut 18:20).

In conclusion it should be noted again that Samuel fulfilled a crucial role as Yahweh God progressively revealed his will for the covenant people. They were to be a kingdom. They were to obey and serve their covenant Lord in the midst of the nations that surrounded them. This became more obvious as David reigned and received assurances from Yahweh concerning his and his descendant's role in the plan and purposes of Yahweh God that would be progressively revealed and worked out.

Progress of Revelation in the Period of David and Solomon's Reign

I. Introductory Comments

The historical record concerning David's experiences during the time between his first anointing (1 Sam 16:1-13) and his second anointing when he actually became king over all of Israel (2 Sam 2:1-5) does not include a reference to Yahweh God speaking to David directly or through a prophet.[1] There is, however, the statement that Yahweh was with David (1 Sam 18:12). David was conscious of this for he said that as surely as Yahweh lives he delivered me out of all trouble (2 Sam 4:9).

David demonstrated that the presence of Yahweh God in the royal city, specifically in the tent he had erected, was of great importance to him. It gave him the opportunity to offer sacrifices, to publicly bless the name of Yahweh of Hosts[2] who had called, protected him, and had him anointed as king over the covenant people

II. Revelation to David

A. By Nathan the Prophet

1. Concerning a Royal House and Kingdom

Nathan is introduced as a prophet in the time of David's reign. David addressed him concerning his problem. He was living in a palace but Yahweh

[1] There is a reference to Yahweh speaking to David when he sought "the face of the Lord" concerning Saul's killing of the Gibeonites (2 Samuel 21:1).

[2] The phrase *besam Yehwah seba'ot* stressed the truth that Yahweh, the covenant Lord, was truly the almighty one who reigned over all.

God's ark, symbol of the divine presence, remained in a tent. Nathan encouraged him to do what he had in his mind. This was not Yahweh's word to David. Nathan was instructed to relate to David what Yahweh's plan was (2 Sam 7:1-4). Before the specifics of the plan were mentioned, Yahweh God reminded David, via the prophet, that he had never requested a house of cedar. Yahweh God had been with his people wherever they were in their journeys. David was also reminded that Yahweh God had taken him from pastures with sheep to be ruler over his people (7:5-8). Then David was promised that his name would be made great (7:9). This had also been promised to Abraham (Gen 15:2). In reality, the promise to Abraham would be realized to a greater extent than before. David, of the tribe of Judah, who had been referred to as the one from whom the *Ruler* was to come (Gen 49:8-12) would be an agent in the progressive revelation and out-working of Yahweh God's plan concerning the seed of the woman (Gen 3:15).

The promise to David specified how Yahweh God would provide a future for his covenant people. Yahweh would establish a house, a royal family, for David. That meant Yahweh would establish a kingdom over which David's descendant would reign. And this descendant would build an earthly house (temple) as evidence that he indeed was the chosen one. He was to demonstrate the progress in Yahweh God's revelation in regard to the seed of Adam being the great victorious one.

Recapitulate: Yahweh God's Promise

a. To Adam that his seed would triumph
b. To Shem, son of Noah, that he was to carry the seed line
c. To Judah that he would be the seed line bearer
d. To David, of the tribe of Judah, that he would be a head in the seed line extending into the future
e. That Jesus Christ, descendant of David, would come in time to fully establish the royal house and eternal kingdom.

2. Concerning His Son

The account of David's adulterous relationship with Bathsheba and the arrangement for her husband's death is well known (2 Sam 11). David, man after God's heart, was a sinful man who defied Yahweh God's will. Nathan was sent to David again. He led David to confess his sin (2 Sam 12:13; Ps 51). He received assurance that his sin was forgiven ("taken away"). David, however, receiving a gracious pardon, nevertheless had to experience the results of his sin. His child with Bathsheba would die (12:13b). Yahweh God had also made known to David that as a result of his sin calamity would come upon his house (12:11-12). And in time David did experience tragedies in his own family.[3]

Yahweh God, who knew the heart of David,[4] revealed his forgiving grace to him. The Lord, however, also revealed his righteousness and justice. David had to remember and know that he was not exempt from these.

B. By the Prophet Gad

The historical situation in which Gad was commanded to make Yahweh's will known to David was after he had taken a census of the covenant people. Gad reported that God gave David three options—all of which were to bring judgment on Israel (2 Sam 24:1-12) and his readiness to stop a plague when David built an altar and sacrificed. Again, justice and grace were revealed and demonstrated.

III. David's Psalms

It is well known that the Psalms are the believing poets' responses to previous or preceding revelations. The psalmists indicated that they knew and believed what Yahweh God had revealed in word and deed. There are, however, a number of references to the psalmists' assurances that Yahweh God had spoken.

Psalm two (2) records that Yahweh in anger rebukes the unbelieving scoffers. He is quoted as saying he has installed his king—his son—who will rule and dash his opponents. Yahweh God is quoted as saying he will arise and protect his people from those who malign them (Ps 12:5). In various Psalms Yahweh God's non-verbal revelation is referred to as his voice in nature (29:3-9). David praises Yahweh God for instruction regarding divine guidance (32:8). Thus he reveals his love (37:28) and gives help and deliverance (37:40; 54:4). Yahweh is extolled because he has revealed himself as man's refuge and strength and fortress (46:1-11). Asaph sang that the Mighty One, God Yahweh, speaks and summons the earth and the heavens to proclaim his righteousness (50:1-7).

A review of the Psalms reminds the reader that the psalmists knew that what Yahweh God had revealed in the past was for their present time and for the future. It must not be forgotten that David knew the sovereign Lord

---

[3] Cf the accounts of Amnon (13:1-19) and Absalom (2 Samuel 13:23—15:12).

[4] In various instances Scripture records that Yahweh God knew the heart of David. Cf. for example, 1 Samuel 16:7.

had enthroned him and had positively spoken concerning David that his descendent would sit at Yahweh God's right hand (110:1-4)

A refrain, expressed in various ways, can be said to be summarized in the words of Psalm one hundred thirty-five (135) verses thirteen and fourteen (13, 14). "Your name O Yahweh endures forever, your renown O Yahweh, through all generations. For Yahweh will vindicate his people and have compassion on his servants." The psalmists knew and were assured that as time moved on Yahweh God would not undo the past but would continue to be their covenant Lord and progressively reveal this in words and deeds.

IV. Revelation to Solomon

A. Solomon: King by Royal Decree

When David became old and feeble and not able to reign effectively the issue of succession to the throne became seriously problematic. David's older sons Absalom and Amnon, were killed when they tried to occupy the throne as successor to David. Thirteen more sons were born to him in Jerusalem, the fourth was named Solomon (1 Chronicles 14:4). David, on his deathbed, by a royal decree, made Solomon his successor. Adonijah, the oldest living son, had considered himself heir to the throne. In the passages that record the transition from David to Solomon (1 Kings 1:1-24; 1 Chr 29:21-25), there is no reference to Yahweh God speaking directly to and through a prophet that Solomon was to succeed David. The Chronicler, however, wrote that Israel acknowledged Solomon as king before Yahweh and Solomon sat on the "throne of the Lord as king in the place of his father David." The Chronicler added "The Lord highly exalted Solomon in the sight of all Israel and bestowed on him royal splendor." (1 Chr 29:21-25). On the basis of what Scripture records one must conclude that Yahweh God's progressive revelation led to the anointing of Solomon and the firm establishment of his throne in Israel. It is added that Yahweh God was "with Solomon and made him exceedingly great" (2 Chr 1:1).

B. Concerning Wisdom

Solomon had been anointed king over the increasingly expansive kingdom. It stretched from the land of Edom and the border of Egypt in the south (2 Sam 8:14) to the far northern region, the Euphrates river (2 Chr 9:26). Soon after Solomon began to reign, Yahweh God spoke to him in a dream. He was offered a choice, he did not ask for victories nor riches but for a discerning heart to govern Yahweh's people and to judge correctly (1 Kgs 3:5-15). The Scriptures record that Yahweh God was pleased. He then promised Solomon a wise and discerning heart and he was promised riches and honor (1 Kgs 3:10-13). Solomon was also promised long life. Yahweh added that it was expected of the king to be faithful in his walk with Yahweh and to obey all his commandments and statutes (3:14).

The Scriptures record that Solomon did become a world renown wise man. It extended to all the areas of life. His proverbs and songs demonstrate that (1 Kgs 4:32-34) as do the books Proverbs and Ecclesiastes.[5]

C. Concerning Splendor

Reference has been made in the preceding that Yahweh God promised riches and fame to Solomon. He thus was able to build the temple for Yahweh God and a palace for himself. After the temple was completely furnished with the most beautiful and durable furnishings available in the entire cultural area, he brought the "Ark of the Lord's covenant" into the temple (1 Kgs 8:1). The entire account is a record of the building, the furnishings and the dedicatory prayer that includes references to what Yahweh God had given Solomon and made possible for him.[6]

Yahweh God's providential activities in the initial years of Solomon's reign were in a real sense a progressive revelation. What Solomon became and made was entirely new. No person before him or as a contemporary could be compared to Solomon the king. Thus Yahweh God revealed progressively the Christ who was to come. Indeed, king David, of the tribe of Judah, was an ancestor of the promised Messiah. Yahweh God revealed that Solomon, not an ancestor of Christ, but as a type of the Christ, reigned over his kingdom in peace and glory.

D. Concerning Covenant Keeping

Scripture records that Yahweh God appeared to Solomon a second time (1 Kgs 9:1-9). The covenant renewed with David had been renewed with Solomon (3:5-15). This second time Yahweh God had a six-point message that he himself spoke. 1) I have heard your prayer and will have my heart in the temple in which you have placed my name (9:3). 2) You, being and remaining faithful, will have your royal throne established over Israel forever. 3) Israel will be cut off from the land given them should you (Solomon)

---

[5] These books are studied with a biblical theological perspective in *FCTC*, Vol. III.

[6] 1 Kings 5:1—8:66 records the preparations, the furnishing, the Solomonic prayers for the people and the prayer of dedication and actual dedication by sacrificing.

and your sons not observe my commands and decrees and worship other gods (9:6-7a). 4) "I, (i.e., Yahweh God) will reject this temple consecrated for My Name" (9:7b). 5) *Then* Israel will become a byword and an object of ridicule (9:7c). 6) Then people will say that Yahweh has brought disaster upon them for embracing and serving other gods (9:9).

E. Concerning Kingdom Disruption

The kingdom of Israel was well established. It was expansive. Solomon the king was famous. His wisdom exceeded that of any known wise man. Yahweh God had fulfilled his promise to Abraham, Joshua and David. Solomon's ships sailed far and returned with gold (9:26-28). He received rich gifts from other kingdoms (10:10-12, 25).

Solomon did not remain true to the covenant Yahweh God had made with Israel. Yahweh God had forbidden the kings of Israel to acquire many horses (Deut 17:16). Solomon accumulated chariots and twelve thousand horses (1 Kgs 10:26-29). Yahweh God had forbidden Israelites to marry foreign women (Deut 7:3; 1 Kgs 6:11-12). Solomon held fast in love to seven hundred wives of royal birth and three hundred concubines. These women led Solomon astray (1 Kgs 11:3) and his heart was not perfect with his Lord.

In this covenant breaking setting, Yahweh God spoke to Solomon saying the kingdom would certainly be torn away from him and given to his subordinates (11:11). One tribe, Judah, would remain for Solomon's descendants for David's sake (11:12).

In conclusion to this study of Yahweh God's revelation to David and Solomon, the question must be asked: Was Yahweh God's revelation to Solomon progressive as it was to David? The answer is "yes, it was." Revelation to Solomon progressed beyond what was given to David. The kingdom was enlarged. Gifts were given by many nations as they brought tribute. In this context Yahweh progressively revealed the fruit of covenant keeping and obedience. He revealed as never before that his promise given generations before Solomon were fulfilled. Yahweh God also revealed as never before that gifts, riches, power, honor and fame were enduring benefits for faithful covenant servants. Yahweh God also revealed as never before that he keeps covenant even when those he covenanted with did not do so. Indeed, Yahweh God revealed that his kingdom, covenant and promise concerning the Messiah to come did not depend on man. He revealed, rather, that he was faithful to the covenant he had established, irrespective of what an illustrious king, who had done much to demonstrate Yahweh's gracious and beneficial gifts to him and his kingdom, had done.

Yahweh God revealed that his plan and work would progress even in the context of unfaithfulness, disobedience and false worship of idols. No person is essential in Yahweh God's work even though Yahweh God calls, assigns, and employs image-bearers to be his channels and instruments of service.[7]

[7] Cf. what was written concerning Solomon's "clay feet." *MROT*, 321.

Progress of Revelation through Five Early Prophets

I. Prophets During Upheavals in Israel

Samuel had served as a prophet during the time he served as the last "judge" in Israel. Others served, as for example, Nathan in the time of David.

A. A Man of God and Ahijah

A prophet, referred to only as "A man of God" spoke against Jereboam and was killed by a lion when another old prophet living in Bethel misdirected the "man of God" (1 Kings 13:1-32). Ahijah had served in the last days of Solomon (11:29-30) and in the time of king Jereboam (14:12-16). These prophets worked during unsettled times and spoke the word of Yahweh concerning Yahweh's manner of dealing with unfaithful prophets and kings. Ahijah prophesied the downfall of Jereboam's royal family.

B. Jehu the Prophet

The word of Yahweh came to Jehu the prophet. It was against Baasha who had assassinated king Jereboam's son. He took the throne over Israel. He killed all of Jereboam" descendants as had been prophesied by Ahijah (15:29). The word of Yahweh made clear why Baasha was under Yahweh God's judgement. He had followed Jereboam's sinful ways, caused Israel to sin and provoked God's anger (16:1-7). The kings who followed, Elah, Zimri and Omri, were characterized as guilty of disobedience and idol worship. It is written that Ahab, induced by his wife Jezebel, sold himself to do evil in the eyes of Yahweh God (21:25). The wickedness of these Israelite kings set the historic stage for Elijah's presence and work.

II. Progressive Revelation Through Elijah[1]

Elijah was the leading prophet during the reign of Ahab and immediately after his death. It is recorded that the word of Yahweh God came to Elijah and that the Angel of Yahweh spoke to him.

Yahweh God protected Elijah after he had revealed Yahweh's plan to bring in a drought during Ahab's reign (1 Kgs 17:1-5). Then Yahweh had him increase oil and flour for a widow (17:13-14) and raise her dead son. Elijah was commanded to meet Ahab to assure him Yahweh God would end the severe drought (18:1-45). The Mt. Carmel episode took place in this context. Yahweh God revealed his presence through Elijah, and through fire and the water soaked altar and the rain that fell.

An angel appeared to Elijah, provided food and commanded him to eat and prepare for his journey of forty days to Mt. Horeb. Once there, Yahweh appeared to Elijah and commanded him to stand on the mountain and experience a theophany. Yahweh God then spoke to him concerning anointing Jehu as king of Israel (19:1-18) and appointed Elisha to succeed him (19:19-21).[2] Elijah received the word of Yahweh again when Ahab had Naboth killed to gain possession of his coveted vineyard (21:15-19). Elijah pronounced Yahweh's judgment upon the king, who then humbled himself and was told judgment would be postponed until his son became king (21:28).

Another prophet, Micaiah, was also active in pronouncing judgment on Ahab. Micaiah contradicted the advice of other prophets who assumed they spoke Yahweh God's word (22:17-28). Judgment was executed on Ahab for he was killed in battle as had been prophesied (22:24-29).

The angel of Yahweh called Elijah to bring Yahweh's word of condemnation upon "Ahaziah, son of Ahab" (2 Kgs 1:3, 15). Elijah was given confirmation that Yahweh would have him pronounce the death of Ahaziah after he had been injured in a fall. The concluding comment in Scripture concerning Ahaziah is that he died according to the word of the Lord that Elijah had spoken (2 Kgs 1:17).

Elijah, the man, had revealed human weakness at times. Yahweh nevertheless had him serve as his spokesman in strenuous times to powerful people. Yahweh, however, continued to reveal himself by words spoken by Elijah and by various deeds he performed. One must conclude that Elijah was an extra-ordinary man who served as Yahweh continued to dem-

[1] There is one reference to Elijah in the Book of Chronicless (2 Chr 21:12) and no references at all to Elisha.

[2] A prophet prophesied victory for Ahab over Ben-Hadad, king of Aran (I Kgs 20:13-22, 28).

onstrate his covenant love for sinful and rebellious Israel and their kings. Indeed, Yahweh progressively revealed grace and mercy through Elijah. A final act of revelation was the transporting of Elijah from earth without his experiencing death. As Moses had not been buried, neither was Elijah. Yahweh thus revealed that there is a living existence once ones earthly life and work is completed.[3]

III. Progressive Revelation Through Elisha

Elisha was recognized as Elijah's assistant by the leaders of Israel. An officer referred to him as the man "who used to pour water on the hands of Elijah" (2 Kgs 3:11). He also received a double portion of Elijah's spirit (2:9-14). Elisha was a miracle performing prophet. He demonstrated that Yahweh God was a sovereign Lord over all aspects of life; people were raised from death, food was multiplied, unexpected events in nature took place, for example, an axe head floated.

Elisha was a spokesman for Yahweh God. He brought the word of Yahweh God to the starving people in beseiged Samaria that food would be available within a day (7:1). Elisha informed Jehu that Yahweh God had commanded him to anoint him as king (9:6, 12). A final reference to Elisha relates his death and burial. Elisha, even in the grave, communicated life to a man who, when buried, touched Elisha's bones and came back to life.

In conclusion to this brief discussion of Elijah and Elisha's ministries, it is well to note that sinful rebellious Israel received revelation from Yahweh God. As referred to before, Yahweh God continued to reveal progressively that he was the sovereign Lord of life and all aspects of it. Israel grew increasingly rebellious as Yahweh God continued to reveal himself in various ways.

[3] Cf. Luke 9:26-30.

XI

Progress of Revelation from 837–725 BC

I. Introductory Comments

A. Progressive-Orderly Sequence

In this study a serious effort is made to trace the precise order in which Yahweh God revealed himself. He did this by word; he called men to prophesy in his name. The phrase "the word of Yahweh came to . . ." does not always give a precise time or method Yahweh employed to make his word known to prophets. The prophets testified, however, that they had been informed and were aware that Yahweh God's message came to them and they were to proclaim it. It should be added that the word came in various contexts, that is, the word came and was proclaimed with accompanying deeds.

It should be noted that at times there was repetition of what had been proclaimed previously. This was done for reminding and emphasizing as situations demanded this. This reality allows for some difficulty in determining the precise sequence in which prophets spoke. There is much agreement among biblical scholars, especially conservative students, to agree to a great degree on the order this study follows.[1]

B. Disagreements

Not all biblical scholars agree with the sequence Professor MacRae has presented. There is disagreement concerning the time the prophet Joel spoke. There is disagreement concerning the unity of the book of Isaiah. Vocabularies, historical settings, and characteristics of prophets are some

[1] Cf. what A. A. MacRae presented in a chart in which he presented the order prophets spoke and the dates of each. "Prophets and Prophecies." *The Zondervan Pictorial Encyclopedia of the Bible*, Vol. I, edited by M. C. Tenny (Grand Rapids: Zondervan, 1975) 879.

of the criteria employed to present challenges to the sequence that the Scripture presents. It should be added that it must be acknowledged that a few prophetic messages were given by some over a lengthy period of time. This is particularly true of the prophecies of Isaiah, Daniel and Zechariah. Some very critical scholars have dissected and divided other prophetic messages also.

In our discussion of each prophet's message, there will be no references to these disagreements. The messages often given in unique circumstances will be considered.

C. Israel, Judah and Nations

The prophets spoke Yahweh God's word to the divided covenant people. Simeon and Benjamin were closely identified with Judah. The other nine were referred to as Israel. Yahweh had messages for Israel as its spiritual disintegration developed. No kings were faithful to Yahweh God and the covenant. Thus, a message of doom was progressively given.

Judah continued to receive prophetic messages. Not all kings were faithful to Yahweh and in time, none were. Hence the message "The End" (the end of it as a nation) was proclaimed to Judah. As there were prophetic messages presenting the progressive word of Yahweh to the covenant people, there were also words from Yahweh God for neighboring nations and more distant nations because they had a part in the covenant peoples' lives.

II. Joel

A. Introductory Comments

The prophet Joel proclaiming the word of Yahweh God, referred to Yahweh God as in Israel (Joel 2:27), his inheritance (3:2) and for whom Yahweh God would be a refuge and stronghold (3:16). Joel, speaking for Yahweh God, referred to the restoration of Judah and Jerusalem (3:1), whose sons had been sold to the Greeks (3:6). Their sons and daughters in turn would be sold to Judah (3:8) and a glorious future awaited Judah (3:18-20). One must conclude that Joel was aware of the separation of the nations, Judah and Israel, and of their reunion as one people in the future.

B. The Prophetic Agenda

The Book of Joel refers to Yahweh communicating his messages that Joel had to proclaim (1:1; 2:12, 19). As he continued to prophesy he spoke as if Yahweh God dictated the messages. The pronoun I appears at least eighteen (18) times.

In another study Joel's agenda for the prophets following him has been presented.[2] Joel's agenda included the three strands of the Golden Cable and sub-themes that developed these strands: 1) the cosmic kingdom, 2) the creational/redemptive/restorative covenant, and 3) the mediatorial covenant agent. The sub-themes have references to the near future as well as eschatological perspectives. The sub-themes are:

1. Great wonders were and will be wrought in the heavens and on the earth.
2. Warnings of local, national, and cosmic disasters.
3. Calls to repentance, obedience, and trust.
4. People calling on Yahweh will be saved.
5. Assurances of Yahweh God's zealous love.
6. Abundant blessings in the creational natural realm.
7. The coming and presence of the Holy Spirit.
8. The renewing of the people and calling on Yahweh.
9. The preaching of the gospel to all nations.
10. The gathering and return of the covenant people.
11. Judgment on the nations and the inclusion of members of these in Yahweh's people.
12. Assurances of peace.
13. Jerusalem, visited but spared, restored, the symbol of Yahweh's presence, throne, reign, a symbol of the kingdom.
14. Water, living and constant, flowing from the temple in Jerusalem.
15. Yahweh God's presence among his worshiping and serving people will be increasingly realized.
16. The Day of Yahweh when the Kingdom of God is fully realized and consummated.

---

[2] See Gerard Van Groningen, *FCTC*, Vol. II, 25-27.

Joel did not include clear references to the promised mediator of the covenant. Various themes he did present were settings and or fruits of the mediator's presence, work and influence. It must also be added that no prophet succeeding Joel referred to him openly or indirectly. An unavoidable conclusion is that Joel did much to demonstrate the progressive aspects of Yahweh God's revelation to his covenant people.

III. Jonah

Jonah, son of Amittai, was of the tribe of Zebulun. He had presented an encouraging message to Jereboam, the second, (2 Kgs 14:25). Jonah, however, is best known as the prophet sent to Nineveh, capital city of Assyria. Yahweh God had come to him and said, "Go to Nineveh, preach against it because of its wickedness has come up before me" (1:1). This command was repeated to Jonah after he had been spewed out by a whale (1:2—2:10). Yahweh God admonished Jonah when he was displeased that Yahweh God accepted the conversion of the Ninevites (4:4). Jonah was also admonished when Yahweh God spoke to him about being angry that a gourd had died (4:9-11).

Yahweh God revealed that his grace, forgiveness, and mercy extended to people not included genealogically in the Abrahamic covenant. This was progressive revelation.

IV. Amos

Amos, a native of Judah, was a contemporary of Jonah. He was called to prophesy to Israel, Judah and neighboring nations. He proclaimed that Yahweh God's roar, coming from Jerusalem, was to be heard and heeded by all these nations (Amos 3:2-3). Amos spoke of the wrath of God to be visited upon Israel, Judah and neighboring nations because of their wickedness. Amos prophesied clearly and directly as no prophet had done before him. No nation, people, or person was exempt from Yahweh God's wrath against wickedness. Amos, however, was specifically called to bring Yahweh God's specific messages to Israel.

The prophet declared that he had messages from Yahweh God no less than eighteen (18) times. Time and again he indicated that he spoke for Yahweh God personally; consider how often he used the pronoun "I." Amos confirmed, developed, and applied the messages that Israel had heard before.

1. Yahweh God had chosen the people he had brought out of Egypt (3:2)
2. Israel was accused of departing from Yahweh God (3:3-10); living complacently in wickedness (6:1-7), and demonstrating pride (6:8-10), and oppressing the poor and needy (8:3-4).
3. Judgment from Yahweh God by the enemy attacks and victories (3:12-15), and from Yahweh God directly (5:1-3; 6:11-14; 8:9-14, 18-24).
4. Israel, hardened in sin, did not repent in spite of chastisement (4:1-13; 5:6b-13).
5. The need and call for repentance as the way to life (5:4-6a, 14-15).
6. The exile was sure to come (5:27; 7:17; 9:1-10).
7. Israel to be replanted in a secure future (9:14-15).
8. Grace and peace given (7:6) and restoration of the Davidic dynasty and the gathering of nations.

Amos repeated, confirmed and expanded on what had been revealed previously. Namely, Israel's election, Israel to come under judgment, the need for repentance, assurance for the future and the Davidic house to abide.

Three Prophets from 782–695 BC

I. Hosea

A. Introductory Comments

The book of Hosea begins with "The word of Yahweh that came to Hosea" (Hosea 1:1). This introduction is followed by the phrase "When Yahweh began to speak through Hosea, Yahweh said to him" (1:2). There are references to Yahweh speaking to Hosea and Hosea using the pronouns *I* and *my* repeatedly when proclaiming the message given him. There are also references to Hosea interpreting. He called for Israel to return to Yahweh (6:1-3), and spoke to Yahweh God saying "Give them O Yahweh, . . . give them wombs that miscarry . . ." (9:14). The Lord has a charge to bring against Judah; he will punish Jacob according to his ways (12:2-6).

B. Israel addressed

The twelve tribes were no longer referred to as Israel. Nine tribes separated from three (Judah, Simeon and Benjamin) and were known as Israel.[1] The three who remained with the kings of the Davidic dynasty were referred to as Judah. Hosea was from Israel and he primarily addressed Israel in his prophecies. He did refer to Judah twelve (12) times. Hosea proclaimed Yahweh's love for Judah (1:7) but also referred to Judah as stumbling (5:5), having sores (5:13) and being unruly against God (11:12). Yahweh God therefore had a charge against Judah also (12:2).

The basic and main theme of Hosea's prophecies to Israel was the covenant (2:18; 6:7; 8:1). Hosea stated the accusation against Israel boldly.

[1] Hosea often referred to Israel by the name Ephraim. This tribe had had a prominent position in Israel's encampment around the Tabernacle (Numbers 2:18-24). Joshua was from Ephraim as was Jereboam who led in the secession of nine (9) tribes.

Speaking as Yahweh God's spokesman he stated ". . . the people [of Israel] have broken my covenant and rebelled against my laws" (8:1). Hosea went on to proclaim that Israel had rejected what is good, set up kings without Yahweh God's approval. They had made idols of silver and gold for themselves (8:1-5). Hosea proclaimed that Israel, as Yahweh's wife, committed adultery (4:15). This was symbolized, at Yahweh's command, by Hosea taking Gomer as wife who became (or was) a prostitute. The sins of Israel constituted a major portion of Hosea's prophecies. Israel was proven to be a covenant breaker in many ways thus proving that spiritual prostitution was her central and greatest sin.

Hosea proclaimed that Israel, having forsaken her husband (2:2) had gone to Assyria (8:9). Yahweh God, however, would use Assyria as a means of punishment and would rule over them (10:6; 11:5). Israel's exile into Assyria was thus prophesied.

Hosea proclaimed Yahweh God's anger against the priests. He stated, as Yahweh's spokesman, that priests ignored the law of God. Like the people they exchanged the glory of God for things disgraceful. They led the people in covenant breaking (prostitution). They sacrificed on hills and mountain tops. They led men to consort with prostitutes and sacrificed with shrine prostitutes. Hosea also assured repentant people that blessings would abound when their waywardness was healed and they were freely loved (14:4-8).

A reading of the Book of Hosea must impress the reader that Yahweh God was proclaimed as a faithful covenant keeper. Yahweh God's covenant included assurances of punishment for covenant breaking. The heart, however, of the covenant was a bond of love and life. Hosea proclaimed that love and a sure demonstration of it in the restoration of the covenant people. Yahweh God was proclaimed as alluring his sinful wife and that she would call him her husband. He would betroth himself to her forever in righteousness, justice, love, and compassion (2:14-20; 14:9).

II. Isaiah

A. Introductory Comments

The Book of Isaiah presents much material for differing methods of interpretation. The position taken by this author is clearly stated—the prophecy is an integrated whole.[2] The prophecy, however, has been divided as to

[2] For further and detailed information on the Book of Isaiah see *MROT*, 508–666; 2 vol. Note especially the following: the authorship and unity of the Book of Isaiah is maintained

content or according to historical contexts and content. Both approaches are helpful and the discovery and study of the Dead Sea Scrolls has given rise to what has been referred to as the bifid approach.[3]

The authors of the introduction to and comments in notes on the prophecy have written that the book "unveils the full dimension of God's judgment and salvation." The Lord is sovereign in judgment and compassionate in the restoration of his people.[4]

B. Isaiah's Call

Isaiah had a vision. In it he saw Yahweh's God, on a throne, exalted and surrounded by heavenly attendants. When Isaiah heard "Whom shall I send?" he responded "Here am I. Send me." He was commanded to go to the people of Judah with a message particularly for them. The people would not respond to his prophesies; they would be exiled and the land would be wasted. But in the future—the seed would be the stump. The seed and stump referred to the Messiah. Isaiah expanded these aspects of the message he was to proclaim (6:1-13).

C. Isaiah's God-given Messages

The first four chapters related to Isaiah's vision concerning Judah and Jerusalem. Terms and phrases used indicate that Yahweh God was the source of Isaiah's prophecies. "The Lord has spoken" (Isaiah 1:2); "hear the word of the Lord" (1:10); "come now let us reason together says the Lord" (1:18); "the Mighty One of Israel declares" (1:24). This is what Isaiah . . . saw . . ." Yahweh God maintains his abode, his ways and his laws; judgment will be rendered and Yahweh God will have his day (2:1—4:1). The Branch of Yahweh God, the Messiah, will again be present with his blessings (4:2-6). The themes included in the first six chapters were repeated, expanded and applied over Isaiah's sixty years of ministry (758–698 BC)

1. The Branch, the Immanuel to be Virgin born (7:13-15; 32:1-8; 42:1-9; 49:1-7; 50:4-16; 52:13—53:12)
2. Exile to come (31:1-9).

---

and that the entire prophecy is an integrated whole which reveals a progression in theological content as historical circumstances developed as they were prophesied they would, 510.

[3] Ibid, 513–15.

[4] J. Stek & H. Wolf, "Isaiah," in *The NIV Study Bible*, (Grand Rapids: Zondervan, 1985) 1015.

3. Yahweh God's anger with his people (Isa 9:8—10:8; 22:1-25; 28:1-15; 42:18-25; 48:1-22; 50:1-3; 51:17-23; 56:9—57:13).
4. Punishment for nations (7:16—8:10; 9:24-34; 10:5-19; 13:1-22; 14:4—21:17; 23:1-1 7; 46:1—47:15)
5. Remnant of Israel (10:20-34; 14:1-2; 30:19-33; 44:1-23).
6. Eschatological events (24:1-23; 28:16-29; 32:9; 35:10; 49:8-26; 54:1-17; 57:1-13; 60:1—63:6; 65:1—66:32)
7. Aspects of worship (12:1-6; 25:1—27:13; 42:10-17; 52:1-12; 63:7-12)
8. Comfort for the people (37:5-7, 21-35; 40:1—41:29; 55:1-13; 57:14-21).
9. Covenant peoples' ministry (43:1-13; 58:1—59:21).
10. Yahweh's attributes and deeds (there are many references; cf. esp. 43:14-28; 45;1-25)

The prophecies, concerning the promised and sure to come Messiah, reveal a great degree of progression. Yahweh God's concern for his covenant people was progressively revealed even when Yahweh God's messages of anger and punishment were progressively proclaimed.

III. Micah

Micah prophesied in the rural areas of Judah while Isaiah prophesied to the urban areas. The prophetic messages for the rural areas did not differ essentially from Isaiah's except that he did not expand on some of the themes that Isaiah had proclaimed. But he did add some progressive revelation and identified himself as a direct emissary of Yahweh God by his use of the personal pronouns, I and my.

Micah referred to Yahweh's witness against Samaria and Jerusalem. Yahweh would come from his dwelling place as a fire to tread the earth because of the sin of Jerusalem and Samaria (Micah 1:3-7). Micah prophesied "I will bring a conqueror, Assyria, (5:5b) against you" (1:15). He identified who he really represented, namely, the glory of Israel (1:12) who had a plan to bring disaster (2:3).

Micah, speaking for Yahweh accused unjust leaders and false prophets who proclaimed peace (3:1-7). Yahweh had a case against his people (6:2, 9-16).

As Yahweh's spokesman, Micah proclaimed that he, i.e., Yahweh's servant, was filled with peace, with the Spirit of Yahweh and with justice and might (3:8a). This servant, a ruler from ancient times, would come through Bethlehem, David's town. He would be the ruling shepherd (5:1-5a) and be the deliverer (5:6b).

Micah reminded Israel and Judah what Yahweh God demanded; worship, proper sacrifice, to act justly, love mercy and to walk humbly with their God (6:6-8).

Eschatological references were intermingled with messages of punishment and doom and with calls for repentance (2:12-13; 4:1-5, 13; 5:7-15; 7:8-13).

Micah represented and served his Lord whom he proclaimed. Yahweh God is merciful, compassionate and faithful. He pardons sin and forgives transgression (7:18-20). He it is that promises deliverance (2:12-13). He calls and gathers his people to be taught Yahweh's ways and laws. He gives them peace and prosperity (4:1-5).

Five Prophets in the Period before the Exile of Judah

AFTER MICAH had prophesied, there was at least a fifty (50) year period in which no prophetic activity took place. During Micah's ministry, approximately from 758–698 BC, the Assyrian army captured Samaria and exiled the northern nine (9) tribes in 722 BC. Assyria also threatened Judah and Jerusalem. Four minor prophets and Jeremiah prophesied during the last years of Judah as a kingdom.

I. Nahum

The prophet Nahum received a vision concerning Nineveh, the capital city of Assyria. The message received via the vision was for both Judah and Assyria. Specific themes that Nahum proclaimed and developed should be noted.

The character of Yahweh God is described. He is jealous, filled with wrath and takes vengeance. He is slow to anger; he has great power that he sovereignly exercises over all creation and particularly over Nineveh (Nahum 1:2—2:1). Yahweh declared that allies would not be available to aid Nineveh (1:12).

Yahweh God declared "I am against you." If Nineveh meant to conduct warfare against Yahweh's people Nineveh itself would be destroyed. (3:1-19).

In the vision Nahum saw that Yahweh *God* is good; he is a refuge in times of trouble. He cares for those who trust in him (1:7). He will restore the splendor of Jacob (2:2a)

II. Zephaniah

During the period that Josiah son of Amnon reigned Zephaniah prophesied that destruction would come. His prophecies included references to Yahweh declaring and saying judgement would come on Judah, Moab and the Ammonites (Zephaniah 1:3, 10; 2:9; 3:20). Zephaniah also referred to himself, using the pronoun "I" when proclaiming what Yahweh God would do.[1] Themes that Zephaniah proclaimed are as follows.

Yahweh God declares he will sweep everything from the face of the earth (1:2). The great day of destruction, by God's hand, is near (1:4-18).

Yahweh God declares (2:9) that Judah's neighboring nations, Philistia, Moab, Ammon, Cush, and Assyria will also be stricken.

Yahweh God would continue to demonstrate he is the covenant Lord of his people. Zephaniah inserts short messages of hope, restoration, and life even as he stressed that a day of wrath and anguish was pending. He proclaimed "Seek Yahweh, righteousness, and humility" (2:3). When the day of wrath comes, and is past, and restoration has come, the meek, the humble and those trusting in the name of Yahweh will live (3:12-13). This remnant will do no wrong. They will be glad and rejoice because Yahweh God the king has forgiven them, strengthens them, is with them, delights in them, loves them, and rejoices over them with singing.

III. Jeremiah

A. Introductory Comments

Jeremiah, a member of the priestly house (Jeremiah 1:1), was called to prophesy during the thirty-one (31) year reign of Josiah (2 Kgs 22:1). He was the last of the kings of Judah of whom it is written "He did what was right in the eyes of the Lord and walked in all the ways of his father David" (Jer 22:2). The kings who succeeded him did not do what was right in the eyes of Yahweh. Jeremiah had much difficulty and grief as he proclaimed the downfall of the house of David and the exile of the kingdom of Judah. He was forced to join a remnant of Judah that fled to Egypt (43:6) after the Babylonians took many citizens of Judah into exile.

Jeremiah was a covenant prophet. He more than any other prophet referred to the covenant Yahweh God had established with the patriarchs, David, and Israel as a whole. He referred to the ark of the covenant (3:16). He said that the covenant had been broken. The curse of the covenant

[1] Cf. my book, *FCTC*, Vol. II, for a concise study of Zephaniah's prophecies.

would be applied to the covenant breaking people (11:1-17). Yahweh instructed Jeremiah to plead with the people to call on Yahweh to uphold the covenant (14:17-23). The people did not do so; they continued to worship other gods. He also prophesied that the covenant would be renewed (3:31-37; 32:40; 33:21-25).

B. Yahweh God's Interaction with Jeremiah

Jeremiah, when he referred to Yahweh God communicating with him, repeatedly used terms and phrases such as "said," "saying," "word of Lord came to me," and "declares" (NIV). They appear more than thirty (30) times in the first five chapters of the book.

Jeremiah is recorded as speaking to or verbally responding to Yahweh God. He claimed he was only a child (1:6). He replied to Yahweh about seeing signs (1:11, 13). He said the sovereign Lord had deceived him (4:10). Jeremiah spoke of his reactions. My heart is faint, I am crushed, I mourn, horror grips me (8:18—9:2; 12:1-4), everyone curses me (15:10).[2] He added, "O Lord you deceived me" (20:7), but the Lord is with me (20:11) and "cursed be the day I was born" (20:14). He lamented "my heart is broken . . ." (23:9, 13).[3]

C. Progress in Revelation

There are specifically four themes that Jeremiah included in his prophecies that emphasized progress in revelation.

1. The broken covenant is to be renewed. Yahweh God's love will continue (31:3). Yahweh will implant his law in minds and hearts and forgive (31:33-34).
2. Judgment is sure to come. Foreign nations will be Yahweh's instruments but they in return will receive extreme punishment. There will be seventy (70) years of captivity.
3. Restoration is sure to come (30:1-3). The people will be healed and enjoy peace (33:6-9).
4. David's righteous "Branch" will come and reign wisely over the remnant of the flock. He will be known as "The Lord Our Righteousness" (23:1-8).

[2] Cf. the Book Lamentations.

[3] Cf. Jeremiah 50 and 51 for a fuller statement of judgment to be executed on Babylon.

IV. Habakkuk

The prophet Habakkuk was a contemporary of Jeremiah. Commentators have pointed out that Habakkuk did not have a specific prophecy addressed to Israel. He did, however, reveal that he was aware of what the historical and ethical circumstances were in Judah (Habakkuk 1:2-4).

Habakkuk's complaints (1:2-4; 1:12—2:1) were answered by Yahweh. He confirmed what other prophets prophesied, namely, that judgment was coming. Yahweh God would employ large nations as agents of divine judgment. Specifically, as the Assyrian nation had conquered and captured Israel, so the Babylonians would serve Yahweh God to bring judgment on Judah (1:6-11). In response, Habakkuk's second complaint was that the Babylonians were wicked, treacherous, and merciless. The question the prophet had was "How can a righteous God identify with, and use such a nation?" Yahweh God's reply was that once the Babylonians served him and went far beyond the limits Yahweh God had set, Babylon would experience the cup of Yahweh God's disgrace, and violence would overcome that nation (2:1-20; cf. esp. 2:16-17). Yahweh God would execute judgment from his holy habitation (2:20). This reply from Yahweh motivated a prayer of submission and trust by Habakkuk (3:1).

In conclusion, considering the question concerning Habakkuk's contribution to Yahweh's revelation, it should be noted that there was no new revelation. There was no progress in revelation. What that prophecy does do is confirm what was prophesied by previous and contemporary prophetic voices concerning Yahweh's omniscience, sovereignty, and grace. And also, his patience with complaining servants who receive the gifts of submission and truth (3:16-19).

V. Obadiah

There is no certainty among Old Testament scholars concerning the date of Obadiah.[4] The prophecy reflects either an historical invasion by Philistines and Arabs in Elisha's time, or of the Babylonians when they invaded Judah and Edom. The Edomite people, who were descendants of Esau, had gloated and rejoiced over Jerusalem and Judah's devastating experiences at the hands of various nations (Obadiah 12–14). Obadiah confirmed previous revelation and added a progressive aspect. He prophesied that "the day of the Lord is

[4] Commentators have referred to similarities between Obadiah, Jeremiah, and Ezekiel's prophecies against Edom (Obad 35:1-15).

near for all nations." The house of Jacob and of Joseph will continue as fire and flame but Esau, the stubble, will be set on fire and consumed. There will be no "survivors" from the house of Esau (Edom).[5]

[5] The Herodian House that reigned during Jesus and the apostles' times has disappeared from the scene of history.

Progress of Revelation Received in Exile

Two prophets were taken along into captivity. Daniel, as a young man, with three friends who were of noble birth (Dan 1:3) and Ezekiel who was of a priestly family (Eze 1:2). Daniel was in Babylon from 606 BC until the Persian empire defeated the Babylonians. Then Daniel was taken to the Persian court. Both men served as prophets. Daniel is referred to as a prophet in Matthew 24:15. Ezekiel, when called, was told that the rebellious house of Judah would know that a prophet had been among them (Eze 2:5).

I. Daniel

A. The Man, Royal and Prophetic

Daniel is believed to have been born circa 620 BC. He was faithful to Yahweh as a youth and throughout his entire life. He spent all of his adult life in royal courts. Yahweh God spoke through him to the palaces of Babylon and Persia. The text records that Yahweh God gave the four young men knowledge and understanding of all kinds of literature and learning. Daniel was enabled to understand visions and dreams (Daniel 1:17). He demonstrated that he was ten times better in wisdom and understanding than all the magicians and enchanters in the Babylonian court of Nebuchadnezzar (1:20). There are no references in the Book of Daniel as in other prophecies, that Yahweh God spoke to him or the word of Yahweh came to him. Rather Daniel received revelation via visions and specific messengers. The messages thus received had many eschatological aspects included in them.

B. Yahweh God's Progressive Prophetic Messages

1. The mystery of king Nebuchadnezzar's dream was revealed to Daniel in a dream (2:19). Daniel, in response, said that the God of heaven, whom he praised (2:20-23), had revealed the meaning of the dream (2:23, 29). The message: four kingdoms will arise; they will be crushed by a kingdom set up by the God of heaven that will never be destroyed (2:44). A rock would destroy the kingdoms. There is a definite reference here to the Lordship and reign of the Rock—Jesus the Christ.
2. King Nebuchadnezzar's dream of a tree was interpreted to inform him that he would be driven out to the field as a hairy animal. The sovereignty of Yahweh God over strong earthly kingdoms was confirmed (4:34-35).
3. Belteshazzar, son of Nebuchadnezzar, was informed that Yahweh God had numbered his days and another regime would arise—as it did (5:25-30).
4. Yahweh God sent an angel to close the mouths of lions in the den into which Daniel had been cast. As a result of Daniel's preservation, king Darius, not a devotee of Yahweh God, testified to peoples, nations, and men of every language[1] that Yahweh God the ever enduring God had a dominion that would never end (6:26). This definitely was an advancement in proclaiming God" eternal kingdom.[2]
5. Daniel had a dream in which four beasts representing four kingdoms would be crushed and a "progressive" revelation was given. The saints that were oppressed would receive the sovereignty, power and greatness of all kingdoms under the reign of the everlasting kingdom in which all rulers would worship and obey the eternal king (7:26-27).
6. Gabriel, Yahweh's messenger angel, came to Daniel in a vision to explain to him that a time of wrath was to come in the distant future (8:19, 26).

---

1 Cf. what John saw and wrote (Revevelation 5:9-10) concerning all peoples.

2 Solomon, centuries before Daniel, had also referred indirectly to Yahweh's son's reign enduring forever (Psalm 72).

7. Gabriel appeared to Daniel as he prayed to give another aspect of the revelation given before. Jerusalem would be rebuilt and the "Anointed Ruler" (Christ) would appear at an appointed time and confirm the covenant as divinely determined (9:25-27).
8. Daniel received a revelation, causing him fright, of a man who assured Daniel that Yahweh God's people would be victorious even when an earthly king exalted himself (10:1—11:45).
9. Michael, the great angelic prince, would arise and protect all those whose names are written in the "Book" that would be revealed in due time. The resurrection of the saints was assured (12:1-4).

In conclusion to this review of revelations given to Daniel, a few points should be stressed. First, Daniel's visions were given with apocalyptic aspects. This reality has given rise to various eschatological interpretations. Second, it must be noted that Daniel received messages that covered a great span of time—from his present time, to the return of some from exile, to the coming of Christ the Messiah, and to the kingdom of the Christ that would endure forever. There is indeed, much progressive revelation given through Daniel.

II. Ezekiel

A. The Man: Priest-Prophet

What is known of Ezekiel is derived from his book. In 597 BC, he was taken to Babylon during the second exile of people from Judah. In captivity he seemed to have had various opportunities in which he demonstrated his priestly character and role while also serving as a prophet. There are two specific periods in his prophesying activity. He spoke of the capture and destruction of Jerusalem and after this occurred, he became a prophet of hope and future blessings. He received visions, performed symbolic acts, and heard messages, for example, "the word of the Lord" came to him. His personal life was involved in his prophetical work. His wife died and he was commanded not to grieve publicly. The people were thus informed not to grieve over the loss of Jerusalem (Ezekiel 24:15-27).

B. Ezekiel's Prophetic Messages

Some of Ezekiel's messages repeated and confirmed what had been prophesied before. A good example of this is the prophecy against nations (25:1-32; 35:1-15). He was told to prophesy against Israel (6:1) and to proclaim the sure destruction of Jerusalem (9:1). Such messages included references to the temple (8:1—10:23).

Ezekiel spoke repeatedly of the glory of Yahweh God. It was often in the context of the temple and in visions of God and heaven (1:22; 3:12, 23; 8:4; 9:13; 10:4, 18-19; 11:22; 24:25; 28:22; 39:21; 43:2-5; 44:4). Ezekiel, the priest-prophet, progressively revealed Yahweh God's glory before, during, and after the exile and as an ever-enduring attribute of Yahweh God.

Ezekiel demonstrated his wide-ranging knowledge of various facets of life as he progressively revealed how these were involved and used in life. He spoke of the watchman (3:16-21), the razor and sword (5:1-12), baggage for travel symbolizing the exile that was sure to come (12:28), magic charms of foolish false prophets (13:1-23), a burnt vine branch (15:1-8); and a wayward foundling (16:1-4). These were included in his prophecies of judgment to come. When speaking of restoration and blessings he included symbols and figures such as the good shepherd (34:1-16) and of him as judge between the good and bad sheep (34:17-31). He portrayed future life by ever-increasing fresh living water (47:1-12).

Ezekiel was very conscious of the presence and work of the Holy Spirit. The Spirit came into him and lifted him up (2:2; 3:12, 14, 24; 8:3; 11:1, 5; 43:5), and gave him visions (11:24). Yahweh will put the Spirit in One (36:27; 37:14), and he will be poured out (39:29). Ezekiel's proclamations concerning the Holy Spirit were spoken when he prophesied of judgment and of restoration and renewal. He thus gave progressive revelation concerning the coming and work of the Holy Spirit.

Progress of Revelation in the Post-Exilic Era

I. Historical Writings

There are four books that record historical events and relationships. It is believed these were written in the first century after the exile took place.[1] The book Esther, written during the exilic period, records life with its dangers and preservation during the actual period of the exile. It does not include direct revelation from Yahweh God during this period.

Chronicles 1 and 2 were written after the return of a small group from exile. The main purpose for the composition of these historical works was to demonstrate that the post-exilic community was a direct continuation of pre-exilic Israel and Judah. There is no specific revelatory material that could be considered progressive revelation other than to posit a continuation of the people of Israel, Yahweh God's covenant with them, the law given at Sinai and the call for worship with the temple as a major factor for proper worship.

The Book Ezra contains two main parts; Ezra's first return to Jerusalem, the re-building of the temple and the revival of worship. The second part records Ezra's second return to Jerusalem and his reforms.

Nehemiah was basically an administrator who recorded the need for the reconstruction of the walls of Jerusalem and introducing some reforms. He recorded that Ezra's preaching had a salutary result. This led to further reforms that dealt with intermarriage, abuse of the Sabbath and the use of the temple. These writings do not record a progress in revelation. They do strongly confirm the importance and relevance of revelation given to Israel from the time of the patriarchs to the time of the exile.

---

[1] Consult my book, *FCTC,* for a detailed study of the historical background to the context of the three post-exilic prophets, 394–381 BC.

These historical writings proved a context in which three prophets were called to address the returned community.

II. Haggai

The prophet Haggai, according to some interpreters, saw the temple before it was destroyed (Haggai 2:3). If this is correct he was approximately eighty (80) years old when he prophesied to the returnees from the exile who were living in Jerusalem.

Haggai made no less than fifteen (15) references to Yahweh God speaking or causing his word to come to Haggai. Thus the prophet was given important messages to the people in Jerusalem. His messages were not absolutely new. He confirmed that the covenant made with Israel (Exodus 19–24) was still in force and binding. Yahweh assured the people that he was with them and that his Spirit remained among them (Hag 2:4). These realities were stressed as basis for the call to obedience that would be demonstrated in their re-building of the temple before they built their own houses as they were doing. Thus the priority of God's house and the worship of him was stressed.

Haggai's messages included the following themes in addition to the demand for obedience in the unique circumstances. The high priest, Joshua, was called to be strong and faithful (2:4). The Messiah's eventual coming was referred to in a unique manner: "the desired of all nations." Cataclysmic events would take place and glory would be revealed and peace would reign (2:6-10). Zerrubabel was indicated as a harbinger of the Messiah (2:23).

Summing up: Haggai wove progressive revelatory aspects in his prophecies. He stressed the necessity of the house of Yahweh to be built as a harbinger for the appearance of the "desired Messiah." He included natural events that would attend his coming. And in this program Yahweh urged the people to assume their role. Two words, "obedience" and "work" summed up this role.

III. Zechariah

A. Introductory Comments

Zechariah was a young man when he began to prophesy. He was a contemporary of Haggai, at least in his first years of prophesying.[2] In his last

[2] Haggai began to prophesy on the first day of the sixth month of the second year of king Darius' reign (Haggai 2:1) and Zechariah began on the eighth month of the second year of king Darius (Zechariah 1:2).

years of prophesying he was very likely a contemporary of Malachi. The book of Zechariah is divided into five parts: *1)* The call to repentance (1:1-6); *2)* the visions, (1:7—6:8); *3)* the crowning of Joshua (6:9-15); *4)* prophetic messages for Jerusalem (7:1—8:23); *5)* messianic and eschatological prophecies (9:1—14:21). The time span the prophecies referred to stretch from the prophets' time to the second coming of Christ. Thus some apocalyptic aspects are interwoven especially through the fifth part of the book. As in preceding prophecies, not all of Zechariah's messages should be considered "progressive revelation." They do confirm for Zechariah's time what had been applied to people and situations preceding Haggai and Zechariah.

B. The Call to Repentance

Zechariah drew a response from the disobedient returnees from exile when he reminded them of Yahweh God's anger against disobedient forefathers. The appeal to past tragedies set the stage for progressive revelation and the response to it.

C. The Visions

Vision one (Zech 1:7-17): The angel of Yahweh, having received reports of peace from four (4) horsemen who had gone throughout the wicked world, asked Yahweh how long Jerusalem would continue to experience his anger. The response was a confirming word that had been spoken repeatedly before. Yahweh was very jealous for Jerusalem and Zion and comforted chosen Jerusalem.[3]

Vision two (1:18-20): The enemies, represented by horns, would be terrified and thrown down and craftsmen would rebuild Israel and Jerusalem

Vision three (2:1-13): Jerusalem is portrayed as a prosperous protected city to which exiles and nations would come. Yahweh will own and declare Jerusalem as his inheritance. A progressive element is introduced. Yahweh comes to and for all people.

Vision four (3:1-10): The very heart of the gospel in Old Testament symbolism is presented by the exchange of filthy garments for a pure white robe for Joshua, the representative for the covenant people. Satan is rebuked.

---

[3] Cf. Exod 20:5; 34:14; Deut 4:24; 5:9; 6:19; 32:16, 21; Josh 24:19; 1 Kgs 14:22; Ps 78:58; 79:5; Ezek 16:18, 42; 36:6; Nahum 1:2.

Vision five (4:1-14): The Holy Spirit is symbolically portrayed by oil for the lampstands—the people of God who obey and do Yahweh's will and do his rebuilding work.

Vision six (5:1-11): Sin and evil bringing the curse is flown out of the land in a covered basket.

Vision seven (6:1-8; 7:1-8, 23): Four horses representing Yahweh God's agent are to bring peace throughout the earth were seen in this climatic vision.

D. The Crowning of Joshua

The visions presented a progressive revelation of Yahweh God having his city rebuilt and its people purified through the Holy Spirit. The passage portraying the content of the seven visions is concluded by a prophetic act; the crowning of the forerunner of Jesus Christ.

E. The Prophetic Message for Jerusalem

Within the law as given centuries before, for example, fasting was confirmed as well as Yahweh's demands for justice and mercy. Without the latter, fasting is meaningless. Jerusalem will be blessed, as prophesied before if the people speak truth, render true judgment and do not plot evil or swear falsely.

F. Messianic and Eschatological Oracles

In the later years of Zechariah's life he proclaimed more progressive revelatory truths. The former prophecies concerning neighboring nations, who had marauded the covenant people, will come under judgment (Zech 9:1-6); the messianic king will ride humbly into Jerusalem (9:13) and the sovereign Lord would reign victoriously (9:14-17). He will gather, care, and strengthen his people (10:1—11:3). False shepherds will be struck down (11:4-17). In reality, all enemies will be destroyed under Yahweh's watchful eyes. Leaders of Yahweh's people will lead in the consuming of enemies (12:1-9). The pierced Messiah will be seen and a spirit of grace and supplication will be poured out (12:10-14). When the shepherd is struck and sheep are scattered a fountain of cleansing will be opened for the house of David and the people of Jerusalem (13:7-9).

Zechariah concluded his prophecy assuring his hearers (and readers) that the day of Yahweh will surely come. All nations will be gathered to fight the people of God but he, Yahweh God, will fight the enemy. The end result will be that the Lord will reign over the whole earth (14:1-21).

Conclusion: Zechariah's prophecies include confirmations of previous prophecies and he presented many progressive aspects of Yahweh God and the coming Messiah's reign and the blessings flowing from these.

IV. Malachi

The prophet Malachi is considered to have been a contemporary of Nehemiah and of Zechariah in his later years. The historical context can be discerned from what Malachi emphasized. The people, doubting Yahweh's faithfulness, were unfaithful as covenant people. The priests were breaking the "covenant with Levi"; impure sacrifices were being offered in worship contexts. Malachi, whose name means "my messenger," demonstrated that he knew his role. In four comparably short chapters he referred to Yahweh God as the source of his messages at least fifteen (15) times. Malachi confirmed what had been prophesied before but he did add some progressive aspects.

Malachi emphasized Yahweh God's election of Jacob and his rejection of Esau. He stressed the reality of Yahweh God revealing his love and wrath (Malachi 1:2-5).

Yahweh God's name will be great among nations. His covenant people were called to honor and serve their Lord, the great king, by their adoring worship and holy sacrifices offered (1:6-14), and the stopping of robbing God (3:6-13).

Yahweh God would send a curse on the priesthood because they failed to reverence Yahweh's name and give proper instruction thus causing people to stumble (2:1-9).

Yahweh God accused the people of breaking vows made to him and those made in marriage. He hates divorce (2:10-16).

Yahweh God repeated in explicit terms that he would send his messenger of the covenant who would bring judgment on all law breakers but cleanse the faithful (3:1-5).

Yahweh God had Malachi prophesying concerning the "Day of the Lord," a day of purification, a great and dreadful day before the Messiah comes who will be preceded by Elijah (4:1-5).

This progressive prophecy concerning Elijah to come was fulfilled when John the Baptist ministered (Matthew 11:14; Luke 1:17). The greatest progress in Yahweh God's revelation was expressed by John (3:16).

www.ingramcontent.com/pod-product-compliance
Lightning Source LLC
LaVergne TN
LVHW010939100826
845153LV00001B/92
9781498248440